Photo Credits:

© 2012 Discovery Communications, LLC. Discovery Channel and the Discovery Channel logo are trademarks of Discovery Communications, LLC, used under license. All rights reserved. MythBusters and the MythBusters logo are trademarks of Beyond Properties Pty Limited.

www.discovery.com/MythBusters

Published by Scholastic Inc. SCHOLASTIC and associated logos are trademarks and/or registered trademarks of Scholastic Inc.

ISBN 978-0-545-43397-6

12 11 10 9 8 7 6 5 4 3 2 1   12 13 14 15 16 17/0

Designed by Henry Ng and Two Red Shoes Design
Printed in the U.S.A.   40
First printing, September 2012

CONTENTS

INTRODUCTION: TRY THIS AT HOME!

MYTH OR **FACT** ? That's the question the MythBusters try to answer in every episode of the show. Now it's your turn! Once again, we've gone through all the MythBusters experiments and gathered this brand-new collection of myths you can investigate on your own. All of them are safe but fun — you'll learn how to test myths ranging from whether balloons can really lift a kid into the air to whether pirates' eye patches helped them see better at night. If you follow the procedures, you can try these challenging experiments at home and see if you've got what it takes to be a MythBuster.

THE SCIENTIFIC METHOD

Since you're going to be performing science experiments, you should use the scientific method.

- ☑ First, you'll read the myth and find out what materials are needed to test it.

- ☑ Next, we'll give you the steps you need to follow throughout your experiment. Scientists call this the procedure.

- ☑ After the procedure, you'll have a chance to form a hypothesis. A hypothesis is your educated guess about what results you expect to get. Do you think the myth is true? If so, your hypothesis would say so. Think the myth's a fake? Put it all in your hypothesis.

- ☑ Finally, you'll record your conclusion. Was the myth confirmed or busted? Your conclusions should wrap up and convey what you learned.

ON THE FIRST PAGE OF EACH EXPERIMENT, YOU'LL NOTICE SOME TEST TUBES.

If you see one test tube, you'll know the myth is simple and that you can probably investigate it on your own.

Two test tubes means you may need a little help pulling together materials.

If you see three test tubes, you're going to need an adult to help you gather the materials and complete the procedure.

WHAT'S YOUR CONCLUSION?

- ☐ **Confirmed**
- ☐ **Plausible**
- ☐ **Busted**

You're going to need to take notes about your hypothesis and your observations, so keep a lab notebook to make sure you're keeping track of everything you discover.

Cost Calculator: Most of the costs for all of these experiments are low, but there are some that require more equipment than others. At the start of each experiment, you'll see dollar signs. One dollar sign means the equipment you'll need will cost less than $15; two dollar signs means between $15 and $25; and three dollar signs means $25 or over.

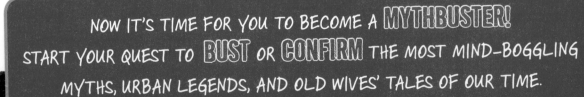

NOW IT'S TIME FOR YOU TO BECOME A **MYTHBUSTER!** START YOUR QUEST TO **BUST** OR **CONFIRM** THE MOST MIND-BOGGLING MYTHS, URBAN LEGENDS, AND OLD WIVES' TALES OF OUR TIME.

DO RATS PEE ON SODA CANS BEFORE YOU BUY THEM, LEAVING BEHIND GERMS THAT CAN MAKE YOU SICK?

WHAT YOU'LL NEED:

- ☐ Two cases of canned soda — one for your control group, one to test for rat pee
- ☐ 1 black light*
- ☐ Cleaning spray
- ☐ Sponges or rags
- ☐ 1 large cloth or towel to cover the clean cans
- ☐ 1 roll of masking tape
- ☐ 1 marker
- ☐ Optional:
    - 1 rat**
    - 1 aquarium, minimum 10 gallons
    - 1 camera***

Are there rodents running around behind the scenes at your favorite snack shop, leaving little presents on your soda cans? That's the idea behind this myth. Some people believe that carelessly stored cans are exposed to rodent excrement that carries disease, and that you can become infected you when you drink from them.

Jamie and Adam had access to a mass spectrometer that was able to indicate the presence of rodent pee. You probably don't have one of those, but if you follow the steps below, you'll get a pretty clear idea of the truth in this situation.

*Black lights can be purchased at hardware stores or online. Small, handheld lights start around $7.

**It isn't necessary to perform the experiment with a rat-pee control as Jamie and Adam do on the show. You can do this without the rats. However, if you do decide to use a rat-pee control, you may be able to perform this control at a pet store without purchasing a rat. If you purchase a rat for the experiment, remember that you are now responsible for a living creature. This rat is now your pet, and pet rats can live more than 5 years.

***The camera is optional. It's a good way to record data from your tests.

TIME REQUIRED:
2 hours for exposure of control if using rats; several days or weeks to store clean cans; a few hours to collect cans from various stores; 10 minutes to collect and compare data

WHAT TO DO:

STEP 1 First, you need to observe what is illuminated on a clean set of cans, to make sure that your black light reveals only rat pee. Create a control group of cans and spray the top of each can using your cleaning spray and sponge. When the cans are clean and dry, darken the room and shine the black light on the top of the cans. If you see anything, make a note of it — these cans are clean, so that means even clean cans may show some matter that isn't rat pee. Cover the cans with a cloth or towel to keep them clean.

STEP 2A Now you need to make a decision. You can compare your test cans to 1 of 2 types of controls: The first is the more precise and involves the presence of actual rat pee; the second is to compare your tests to a sample that has been sitting in storage but with absolutely no exposure to rat pee.

If you decide to create a rat-pee control, you'll need to have access to a rat (or if you or someone you know has a pet mouse, hamster, or gerbil, you can use any of these small rodents instead; the results will be close enough). The simplest way to do this is to perform the test in a pet store where you've been given permission to let a rat run around on your cans for a while. If you decide to use a rat you've purchased as your own pet, you can do this at home.

Fill the bottom of your aquarium with your cleaned soda cans, so the floor of the aquarium is completely covered. Place one or more rats into the aquarium and let them be for 1 1/2 – 2 hours. At the end of that time, remove the rats, darken the room, and use your black light to illuminate the cans. Make a note (or take a photo) of what the urine puddles and splotches look like. These are the marks you'll be looking for on your test cans.

STEP 2B If you're not working with live rats, or even if you are, it can be helpful to observe cans that have not been cleaned but also have not been exposed to rat pee. Use your black light to observe cans you've stored someplace with absolutely no signs of rodents, or by keeping at least one case of exposed canned beverages in storage in a place where rats will not have access to them. Use your black light in a dark room to see if there are any marks on the cans that haven't been cleaned but are also free of rat pee. Make a note or take a photo of these cans for comparison to your test cans.

STEP 3 It's time to collect your test cans. Go to as many different stores as you can and purchase at least one soda can. Use the masking tape and marker to label each can with the location where you purchased it (if you find rat pee, you'll know to avoid that store in the future!). Once you've collected as many cans as possible, use your black light to observe the tops. Make notes of your observations or take a photo to record the results.

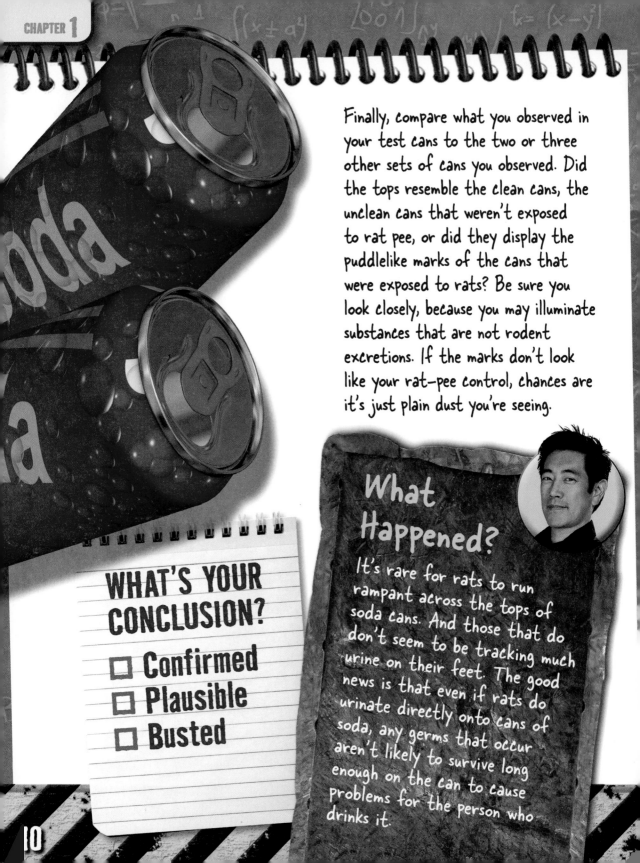

Finally, compare what you observed in your test cans to the two or three other sets of cans you observed. Did the tops resemble the clean cans, the unclean cans that weren't exposed to rat pee, or did they display the puddlelike marks of the cans that were exposed to rats? Be sure you look closely, because you may illuminate substances that are not rodent excretions. If the marks don't look like your rat-pee control, chances are it's just plain dust you're seeing.

WHAT'S YOUR CONCLUSION?

☐ **Confirmed**
☐ **Plausible**
☐ **Busted**

What Happened?

It's rare for rats to run rampant across the tops of soda cans. And those that do don't seem to be tracking much urine on their feet. The good news is that even if rats do urinate directly onto cans of soda, any germs that occur aren't likely to survive long enough on the can to cause problems for the person who drinks it.

TRY THIS:

USE A BLACK LIGHT TO CHECK YOUR HOME AND SCHOOL FOR UNSEEN NASTIES.

WHAT YOU'LL NEED:

☐ 1 black light

TIME REQUIRED: As much as you want!

WHAT TO DO:

Now that you know what rodent excretions look like (if you didn't try this at home, watch the episode where Adam and Jamie run the experiment . . . yuck!), use your black light to check around your home for signs of rambunctious rodents. Shine the light under your sinks, inside cabinets, and in corners behind furniture. Look for the telltale puddlelike marks that piddling rodents leave behind. You can also check around your toilet for leaks, or on doorknobs or light switches for signs that other germy substances are lurking. If you can get permission, check your friends' homes, around school, or where your parents work. You'll be amazed by everything you can discover with nothing but a black light!

DO SOME FOODS MAKE YOU GASSIER THAN OTHERS?

Are beans a food that's best saved for the great outdoors? Will soda bubbles come out in the same form they go in? Does meat make more melodious music than grains or veggies? Adam, Jamie, and Kari were determined to find out if these claims are true or just stinky rumors.

WHAT YOU'LL NEED:

☐ 3 small pocket-sized notebooks
☐ 3 pencils
☐ 2–3 cans of beans
☐ 1–1 ½ lbs of meat
☐ 4–5 cans of carbonated water
☐ Graph paper
☐ Two partners*

*You can do all the data collection by yourself if you want — you'll just need to leave some extra days for the change in diets. If you work alone, give yourself at least 24 hours of normal diet between testing each of the foods to prevent overlap of gas production from different trials.

TIME REQUIRED:
4 days, plus a couple hours to compile data

WHAT TO DO:

STEP 1 ▶ Decide when you'll have 3 days during which you can keep track of the amount of gas (or *flatus*) you and your 2 partners normally produce. This will be your control period. Each person should have a notebook and pencil to record the number of flatus he or she produces over the 3-day period. Make sure each day is a full 24 hours. During that time, don't consume beans, carbonated beverages, or much meat.

If you want to get more technical with your data, you can create a data sheet that allows you and your partners to differentiate between different types of flatus. Create a chart with a row for each day and label 3 columns at the top of the page with the following:

Single Pop	Multiple Pop (Under 1 Sec)	Long (More than 1 Sec)	Total Score

For 3 days, have each person keep track of the number of times he or she passes gas. If you're using the more specific data chart, each person should make a mark under the appropriate column for 3 days. Assign 1 point for each single pop, 2 points for each multiple pop or short burst, and 3 points for flatus that lasts longer than 1 second. Add up these points under the total score column.

STEP 2 At the end of the 3 days, find the average normal flatus for a person by adding up the number of flatus and dividing it by 3. If you're using the scoring chart, add the 3 total scores and divide by 3.

STEP 3 Now it's time to test the effect of different foods. Decide who will be testing each diet and determine what 24-hour period you will use for data collection. Start the 24 hours at a mealtime, like breakfast. Each person should use either his or her notebook or a clean copy of the data sheet.

Each person should consume significantly more of the food he or she is testing over the 24 hours. The bean eater should consume at least 1/2 to 1 cup of beans at every meal, the meat eater should eat a serving of meat at every meal, and the carbonated beverage drinker should drink at least 12 ounces of carbonation at each meal and once in between meals.

STEP 4 At the end of the 24 hours, add up the number of flatus or flatus points each person counted and compare it to the average from the first 3 days. What do you think? Are beans, soda, and meat guilty of creating gas galore?

WHAT'S YOUR CONCLUSION?

☐ Confirmed
☐ Plausible
☐ Busted

What Happened?

There are 2 ways we can get gassy: by swallowing gas that makes its way all the way through us, or by having bacteria inside our gut produce gas. That's right — we have billions of bacteria living inside us, just waiting to snack on the food we don't digest. We benefit from the bacteria because they digest food we can't, like the cellulose in vegetables, and, as a result, we get more vitamins out of those foods. But they produce carbon dioxide in the process.

The harder a food is for us to digest, the more food the bacteria get. Beans have a lot of fiber and a tough seed coat. Those can be hard for us to digest, creating a feast for the bacteria — and more gas for us!

DOES BEING SCARED REALLY GIVE YOU COLD FEET?

If you're afraid to do something, you might be accused of having cold feet. But does the temperature of your feet really change when you're scared? Kari, Grant, and Tory went to some pretty crazy extremes to scare one another. But have no fear, we've got some creepy (but safe!) ideas for you to try at home!

WHAT YOU'LL NEED:

☐ 1 thermometer*
☐ Several willing test subjects
☐ 4–5 harmless but scary-looking insects or worms**
☐ 1 notebook
☐ 1 pen or pencil

TIME REQUIRED:
30 minutes and up

* There are 2 different options for the type of thermometer to use in this experiment. The first is to use ThermaDot disposable thermometers, which can be purchased at the drug store for about $15 for a pack of 100. If you use these, you'll need to use a thick sock or pillow to hold the thermometer onto the foot you're testing to insulate it from the air temperature, and you may want to take several readings to get the most accurate reading possible. Another option is to purchase an infrared thermometer that takes temperatures without actually making contact with the test subject. These thermometers can be purchased online for around $65.

** It is only advisable to use situations that might seem scary to some people, but that are completely safe in reality. A recipe for bugs you can eat is on page 19. DO NOT feed a person with shrimp allergies bugs of any kind.

WHAT TO DO:

STEP 1 The most challenging part of this experiment is figuring out how to scare your test subjects safely. We recommend using insects or bugs. It should be easy to find a friend who has a phobia of bugs, and you can create situations that may scare them without putting them in any real danger. Harmless insects that you can find without too much difficulty include earthworms, beetles, black ants that don't bite, or daddy longlegs (from a nearby outdoor space); mealworms or crickets (from a pet store). Remember, if you're using insects, you are using living animals and you should be prepared to free them or feed them to another pet when you're finished. Do not intentionally cause harm to the animals you use in your experiment.

STEP 2 Once you have your scary situation set up, it's time to test your first subject. Get your friend settled into the location you plan to test him and take an initial foot temperature reading. Taking more than one reading and averaging the temperatures will give you the best possible data. Record this information in your notebook.

STEP 3 Now for the fun part: scaring your subject! If you are using insects or worms, you might keep them in a clear terrarium and simply put the bug container in front of your subject. Some people might tolerate having the bugs placed in their hands or even placing their hands into the container with the bugs.

STEP 4 Once your subject is good and scared, keep the scare tactic in place and take your second temperature reading. Once again, using the average of several readings will give you the most accurate data.

Compare your first and second readings. What do you discover? Did your subject's feet get cold, or is this myth full of hot air?

WHAT'S YOUR CONCLUSION?

☐ **Confirmed**
☐ **Plausible**
☐ **Busted**

What Happened?

When people get scared, it initiates a hormonal response called the fight or flight reaction. Your body gets ready to fight a danger or run away by drawing blood from your extremities into your main muscles and organs. This way, the most important parts of your body have the energy they need to help you out. As a result, blood moves away from your hands and feet, which can result in a decrease in temperature.

TRY THIS:
CRITTER COOKBOOK

Eating bugs was the worst thing Grant and Tory could do to scare Kari when they tested this myth. But plenty of people around the world eat bugs every day. In fact, in some places it's a major source of protein. Here are a couple of recipes you can use to cook up a snack of your own. You can use it in your experiment, or just for after-school treats.

Note: The crickets and mealworms roasted in these recipes can be used for any recipe you want, or even eaten on their own (maybe with a little salt . . .).

WARNING:

Ask an adult to help you perform this experiment. You should not use the stove by yourself without permission from a parent or teacher.

TIME REQUIRED:
About 2 hours

CHOCOLATE-COVERED CRICKETS

INGREDIENTS:
- ☐ 20 live crickets (can be obtained from your local pet store or online supplier)
- ☐ 1 bag of semi-sweet chocolate morsels

STEP 1 ▶ Prepare your crickets. Working with live crickets can be challenging, but fortunately, it's easy to put them to sleep. Place the crickets in a plastic bag and put the bag in the freezer for about 20 minutes. When you take the bag out, the crickets should be immobile. Place the sleeping crickets in a colander, cover them with a thin cloth or paper towel (in case they wake up), and rinse them with cold water. Pat them dry with another cloth or paper towel, return them to the bag, and place them in the freezer for another 10 minutes.

STEP 2 ▶ Spread the crickets on a baking sheet. Ask your adult to help you place them in the oven, and then roast them at 200 degrees Fahrenheit for about an hour, until they're crunchy when you pinch them between your fingers. If you test them and they're not crunchy, give them a few more minutes in the oven. Then take them out again and let them cool for 15 minutes.

STEP 3 ▶ While the crickets cool, ask your adult to help you melt the chocolate in the top of a double boiler. Use tweezers to dip each cricket into the chocolate until it's covered completely. Place the crickets on a sheet of wax paper to cool, and then enjoy!

MEALWORM BANANA BREAD

INGREDIENTS:

- ☐ 3 very ripe bananas
- ☐ 1/3 cup softened butter
- ☐ 1 cup sugar
- ☐ 1 egg, beaten
- ☐ 1 teaspoon vanilla
- ☐ 1 teaspoon baking soda
- ☐ 1/4 teaspoon salt
- ☐ 1 1/2 cups all-purpose flour
- ☐ 1/4–1/2 cup live mealworms

$$

WARNING:

Ask an adult to help you perform this experiment. You should not use the stove by yourself without permission from a parent or teacher.

TIME REQUIRED: About 2 hours

WHAT TO DO:

STEP 1 Place the mealworms in a colander and rinse them with cold water. Pat them dry with a dishcloth or paper towel and place them in a plastic bag. Put the bag in the freezer for an hour. Then spread the mealworms on a baking sheet and ask your adult to help you roast them at 200 degrees Fahrenheit for an hour, or until they are crunchy when pressed between your fingers.

STEP 2 Preheat your oven to 350 degrees Fahrenheit. Mix together the ingredients for the batter. Using a large spoon, first combine the butter and the bananas. Next add the egg, sugar, and vanilla. Then add the baking soda and salt. Mix in the flour and, finally, carefully stir in the mealworms, being careful not to break them up too much.

STEP 3 Pour the batter into a 4 x 8 loaf pan and bake it for 1 hour, or until a fork inserted into the middle comes out clean. Let the loaf cool at least slightly before slicing.

TRY THIS: MAKE YOUR OWN JAWBREAKER CANDY.

Urban legend says that if you heat a jawbreaker in a microwave for the right amount of time, the middle will melt while the outside stays hard. Then, when an unsuspecting kid takes a bite of his sweet treat, the cool outside will crack open and the molten insides will burst out, causing major burns on the inside of your mouth. This is another tale that's too dangerous to test, so you'll have to take the MythBusters' word for the fact that it's plausible. But you can also make your own jawbreaker — without it exploding!

WARNING:

Ask an adult to help you perform this experiment. You should not use the stove by yourself without permission from a parent or teacher.

WHAT YOU'LL NEED:

- ☐ 8 cups sugar
- ☐ Liquid hard-candy flavorings✱
- ☐ I package of food coloring
- ☐ Water
- ☐ I pot
- ☐ I muffin tin — large or small will work
- ☐ 5-6 foil muffin liners
- ☐ I set of measuring spoons
- ☐ I measuring cup
- ☐ Nonstick cooking spray
- ☐ Candy thermometer✱

✱ You should be able to find candy flavorings and a candy thermometer online if you can't find them at a local store. Your candy will be a little more exciting with added flavor and color, but you can make a plain jawbreaker if these ingredients are too difficult to get your hands on.

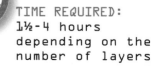

TIME REQUIRED:
1½-4 hours depending on the number of layers

WHAT TO DO:

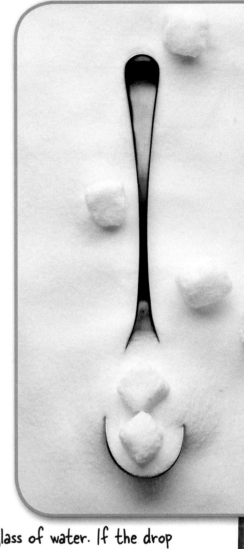

STEP 1 ▶ Line your muffin tins with the foil liners, and then coat them lightly with the nonstick cooking spray.

STEP 2 ▶ Mix 1 cup of water and 3 cups of sugar together in a pot. Put the pot on the stove top and turn the heat to High. Add 2 teaspoons of a flavor and color you want to use. Stir the mixture constantly as the sugar melts.

STEP 3 ▶ Use the candy thermometer and heat the mixture until it reaches 295 degrees Fahrenheit. Ask your adult to help you, and be extra careful, because it will be VERY hot! The candy needs to be this hot or it will not harden fully. If you don't have a thermometer, you can test the readiness by dropping a small amount of melted sugar into a glass of water. If the drop hardens after a few seconds, the mixture is ready. If it doesn't harden completely, continue heating and repeat the test until the sugar hardens in the water.

STEP 4 Divide the mixture evenly among your foil liners. Let this first layer cool for about 30 minutes. Putting the tray in the refrigerator is a fast way to cool it down.

STEP 5 Repeat steps 2 and 3 until you have as many layers on your jawbreaker as you'd like.

STEP 6 When your last layer is cool, peel the foil away from the candy. You now have a sweet treat that should last for hours (and definitely won't explode in your mouth!).

ARE THE STUNTS MACGYVER PULLED OFF ON HIS TV SHOW REALLY POSSIBLE?

Jamie and Adam wanted to see how they measured up to MacGyver when it comes to achieving impressive results with whatever materials are at hand. MacGyver gets things done in seconds. Jamie and Adam had a full hour, and they did pretty well overall. Here's a challenge you can try at home. Next time you're lost in the woods with a magnet and a piece of metal, you'll know exactly what to do to get your bearings!

TRY THIS:

MAKE YOUR OWN COMPASS.

TIME REQUIRED:
15 minutes

Note: You can also magnetize your compass needle with a battery and copper wire by following the directions on page 101 of the first *MythBusters Science Fair* book.

WHAT YOU'LL NEED:

- ☐ 1 needle, paper clip, or thin nail
- ☐ 1 kitchen magnet (the stronger the better)
- ☐ 1 shallow dish or cup that's wider than the metal object you plan to use
- ☐ 1 cork
- ☐ 1 pair of scissors

WHAT TO DO:

STEP 1 Magnetize your needle by stroking it in one direction with your kitchen magnet. Do this about 20 times, and then put the original magnet away.

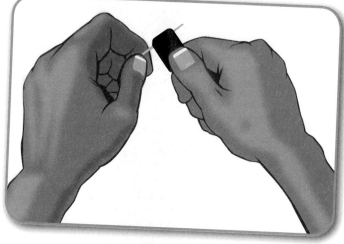

STEP 2 Using the scissors, cut a circle about 1/4–1/2 inch thick from one end of the cork. Ask an adult if you need help.

STEP 3 Push the needle through the middle of the cork piece (running horizontally through the cork) so that it sticks out evenly from both sides. When you hold it up, it should look like a circle with a needle through it.

STEP 4 ▶ Fill the cup or container half-full of water and place the cork in the water so the needle floats at the top. This is your compass! Place it on a flat surface away from any other magnets and see what happens. If you have a scientific compass, you can compare it to see how accurate your homemade compass is. You can also try placing another magnet near your compass and see what effect this has on your needle.

What Happened?

The Earth creates a magnetic field that runs between its poles. This field will cause other magnets that are free to rotate (and not affected by other closer or stronger magnets) to line up so they're parallel with the Earth's magnetic field.

TRY THIS: MAKE YOUR OWN CANDLE.

The MythBusters tested whether it was possible to make a candle with earwax. In order to collect enough wax to make a full candle, the team had to gather the earwax of many people. And once they'd done that (a pretty gross endeavor — and dangerous, too: You should never stick anything smaller than your elbow in your ear), the candle they produced hardly even burned. So here's an idea for something similar that's fun and safe enough to try at home.

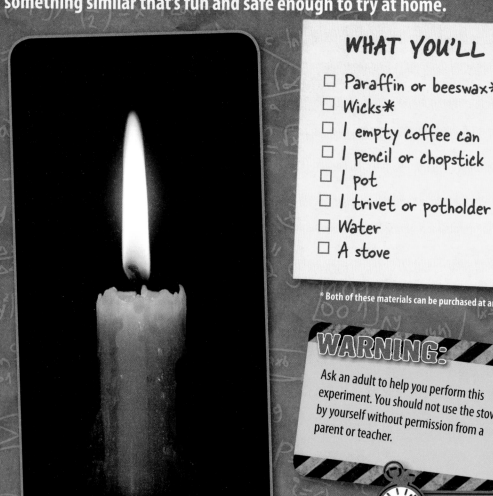

WHAT YOU'LL NEED:

- ☐ Paraffin or beeswax ✳
- ☐ Wicks ✳
- ☐ 1 empty coffee can
- ☐ 1 pencil or chopstick
- ☐ 1 pot
- ☐ 1 trivet or potholder
- ☐ Water
- ☐ A stove

* Both of these materials can be purchased at arts and crafts stores.

WARNING:

Ask an adult to help you perform this experiment. You should not use the stove by yourself without permission from a parent or teacher.

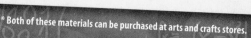

TIME REQUIRED:
90 minutes

WHAT TO DO:

STEP 1 ▶ Place the beeswax or paraffin in the coffee can, and then put the can into the pot of water (a double boiler would be perfect). With an adult's help, heat the wax on low to medium heat until it is completely melted.

STEP 2 ▶ While the wax is melting, cut your wick. You'll want to cut it about 6 inches longer than you want your candle to be. Tie one end of the wick to the pencil or chopstick.

STEP 3 ▶ When the wax is fully melted, ask the adult to remove the pot from the stove and place it on a trivet on a working surface. Holding the pencil or chopstick, dip the free end of your wick into the wax quickly; the length of wick you cover with wax will be the height of your candle. You want only a thin layer of wax to be added at a time. Be very careful as you do this, or ask your adult for help, as the wax can be quite hot.

STEP 4 ▶ Let the wax on the wick cool completely, and then quickly dip the wick again. Continue dipping and cooling your candle until it reaches the thickness you're looking for.

STEP 5 ▶ When you've added your last layer of wax and it has cooled completely, trim the wick to less than half an inch. Place the candle in a holder, and enjoy!

TRY THIS: MAKE YOUR OWN PAINT.

Painting a house with dynamite is a myth best left to the professionals to test. Using potentially explosive components to make house paint may sound fun, but it's more difficult than you might think. Consider the first step: get some dynamite. But if you're feeling creative, here's something that's fun and safe enough to do at home.

WHAT YOU'LL NEED:

- ☐ Several spices with strong pigments, like turmeric, paprika, and curry or chili powder
- ☐ Finely crushed powdered chalk
- ☐ Charcoal powder
- ☐ 1 carton of low-fat cottage cheese
- ☐ Water
- ☐ Baking soda
- ☐ 2–3 egg yolks separated from the white
- ☐ 5–6 aluminum foil muffin cups or baby food jars
- ☐ 2–3 paintbrushes
- ☐ Thick paper, cardboard, or scrap pieces of wood
- ☐ 1 set of measuring spoons

TIME REQUIRED:
30 minutes, plus overnight for binders to form

WHAT TO DO:

We've got 2 different kinds of paint you can try making. Both involve pigments and a binding agent. Pigments are colorful materials like charcoal, chalk, and spices. You can try all kinds of things with color as your pigments — we've included just a few ideas to get you started. In this experiment, we use two binders: cottage cheese and egg yolk. The milk protein in cottage cheese binds the pigment in one, and the egg yolk binds in the other.

STEP 1 In a muffin tin or baby food jar, mix 1 tablespoon of low-fat cottage cheese with 1 teaspoon of baking soda and 1 tablespoon of warm water. Let this mixture sit for an hour, stir it well, and then let it sit overnight. When you come back, stir the mixture. It should become smooth and clear — the baking soda will break down the lumps in the cottage cheese.

STEP 2 Choose which pigment you'd like to use and divide the binder into different cups. Add pigment until you get the saturation of color you want. If the paint is too thick, add some water to thin it out.

STEP 3 ▶ Use a paintbrush to apply the paint to a piece of paper or wood. This paint is water soluble, so you can clean your brushes with water from the sink.

STEP 4 ▶ To make your second binder, mix the egg yolk with a quarter cup of water. When the egg is thoroughly mixed, add the pigment you want to work with. You need to use a lot of pigment for this binder. This paint is called egg tempera. Use a clean brush to try it on your paper. This is another water-soluble paint, so use water when you're ready to clean up.

What Happened?

Applying a pigment to surfaces on its own would add color, but that color wouldn't stay in place; it would wash away as easily as sidewalk chalk. By mixing the pigment with a binder, you're setting the pigment in a substance that will hold the color in place and stick to the surface you've painted. This way, your color stays put!

MYTH

CAN YOU FOLD A PIECE OF PAPER IN HALF MORE THAN 7 TIMES?

This one's pretty easy to try at home — and it's pretty hard to make that eighth fold. The MythBusters figured the problem might be that no pieces of paper have been big enough to allow that elusive eighth crease, and they set out to make the biggest piece of paper ever. Feel free to fold as many sheets of paper as you want to take this one to the test. If you're feeling crafty, you can even make paper of your own.

TRY THIS: MAKE YOUR OWN PAPER.

TIME REQUIRED:
45 minutes plus
drying time

* Your screen needs to be set in a frame to keep it flat. You can use an old door or window screen, or you can use a screen purchased at the hardware store and attached to a smaller wooden frame with tacks. A picture frame or glued pieces of wood work well for the frame. The frame will determine how large your paper is, but remember, it needs to be able to fit into whichever sink, tub, or basin you're using.

WHAT YOU'LL NEED:

- ☐ Old paper products torn into small squares. These could include: printer paper, newspaper, egg cartons, paper bags, magazines, napkins, tissue paper
- ☐ 1 screen in a frame*
- ☐ 1 blender or food processor
- ☐ Water
- ☐ 1 large sink, tub, or basin (must be large enough that the framed screen fits inside it while lying flat)
- ☐ 1 jug of liquid laundry starch (optional)
- ☐ 1 iron (optional)

WHAT TO DO:

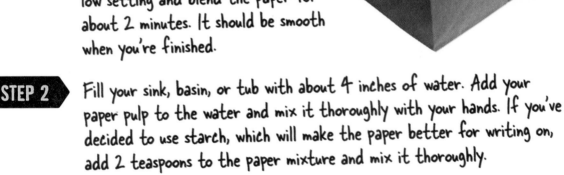

STEP 1 Once you have your paper torn or cut into small squares (no more than 2 inches per side), put them into your blender or food processor. You want the blender about halfway full of paper; fill the rest of the way with warm water. Turn it onto a low setting and blend the paper for about 2 minutes. It should be smooth when you're finished.

STEP 2 Fill your sink, basin, or tub with about 4 inches of water. Add your paper pulp to the water and mix it thoroughly with your hands. If you've decided to use starch, which will make the paper better for writing on, add 2 teaspoons to the paper mixture and mix it thoroughly.

STEP 3 Holding your screen at an angle, submerge it in the paper mixture. Move it around in the water until it appears that you have an even layer of paper particles on the screen. Then, holding the screen flat, carefully lift it out of the water. If it looks like your paper is too thin, make some more blended paper and add it. If it looks too thick, add some water to the mixture. You can take the material off the screen and redo Step 3 as many times as necessary to get the thickness of paper you want.

STEP 4 Hold the frame over the basin and let the water drain off for several minutes. If you have an extra piece of screen, you may want to squeeze it on top of the frame to get rid of extra water. Then place your paper somewhere to dry. You can leave it in the sun or hang it on a clothesline. If you keep your frames inside, make sure they're someplace that won't be damaged by water drips.

STEP 5 When your paper is completely dry, carefully peel it off the screen. If you want, you can ask an adult to help you use an iron on a low setting with steam to smooth out the paper.

LIGHTS ON OR OFF?

Has anyone ever told you to stop flicking the lights on and off because it uses too much electricity? Or told you to leave the lights on if you're going in and out of a room because it uses less electricity than turning the lights on and off? A lot of people believe that the burst of electricity needed to turn on the lights is so big that it uses a lot of energy. But could these people be totally in the dark?

WHAT YOU'LL NEED:

- ☐ 1 pencil
- ☐ Paper
- ☐ 1 calculator
- ☐ 1 digital watt-hour electricity meter* or access to your home's electric meter
- ☐ 1 lamp
- ☐ 1 stopwatch**
- ☐ A partner**

TIME REQUIRED: 20 minutes

*Using a digital electricity meter that you can plug your lamp into directly makes this experiment very simple. The meters can be purchased online or at a hardware store for $25 or less. If you don't want to purchase a meter, you can use a formula and data collected from your home's electric meter.

**You only need the stopwatch and partner if you're using your home's electric meter.

WHAT TO DO:

STEP 1A ▶ First, decide if you're going to use a portable digital meter or your home's electric meter. If you're using the portable meter, find an electric outlet and plug the meter in. Then plug your lamp into the meter. The meter will have a setting that allows you to see how much power has been drawn since you turned it on. Turn on your lamp and leave it for 5 minutes. Afterward, make a note of the reading on the meter to see how much electricity has been used.

STEP 2A ▶ Now comes the fun part. Reset your meter to 0, and then turn the light on and off as many times as you can for 5 minutes. Then take a look at the meter and make a note of how much electricity was used. How does it compare to your first reading? If the second number is much larger than the first, you know you've wasted a lot of energy by flipping it on and off. If the numbers are the same or the second number is smaller, this myth is busted.

STEP 1B ▶ If you're using your home's electric meter, prepare for the experiment by turning off any appliances that can turn on by themselves (like the refrigerator or air conditioners) and make sure everyone at home knows not to change energy usage (by turning on televisions, computers, etc.) while you run your experiment. Choose the light or lights you'll have flicked on and off during the experiment, and make sure they're turned on.

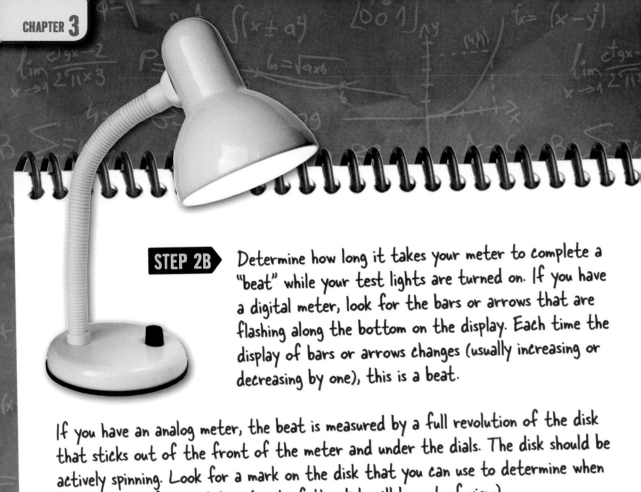

STEP 2B ▶ Determine how long it takes your meter to complete a "beat" while your test lights are turned on. If you have a digital meter, look for the bars or arrows that are flashing along the bottom on the display. Each time the display of bars or arrows changes (usually increasing or decreasing by one), this is a beat.

If you have an analog meter, the beat is measured by a full revolution of the disk that sticks out of the front of the meter and under the dials. The disk should be actively spinning. Look for a mark on the disk that you can use to determine when it has made a full revolution (most of the disk will be out of view).

For accuracy, it's good to use more beats. We recommend using 10 or 20. Start your stopwatch when the digital meter changes, or when the mark you've identified on the disk is in view. Keep it running for 10 or 20 "beats," and then stop the timer. Record this time as Time 1.

STEP 3B You're going to repeat step 2B, but someone else needs to turn your test lights on and off while you do. While your partner switches the lights on and off, take a new measurement of your meter using the directions in the last step. When you've completed the same number of beats, stop your timer and record this time as Time 2.

STEP 4 Compare your 2 times. Was the time with the lights flashing faster than the time when the lights were just on? If so, then you were using more energy. If the times are about the same, then the difference in energy usage is slim.

WHAT'S YOUR CONCLUSION?

☐ **Confirmed**
☐ **Plausible**
☐ **Busted**

What Happened?

It's true that there's a burst of energy when you turn on a light, but it's only enough to run your typical light bulb for a fraction of a second. It would be hard to turn a light on and off enough times to use significantly more energy than simply leaving it on. The bottom line: If you want to save energy, turn off the lights when you leave a room.

TRY THIS: FIND OUT HOW MUCH ENERGY YOUR HOME APPLIANCES USE.

Use this same technique to determine how much energy the lights or any other appliances in your home use. To do this, take your first reading as you did in the experiment, but make sure the appliance (your television, stereo, or computer) is turned off. Take your second reading with the appliance turned on (but with no other changes to electric use). See if your meter has a kH factor. If it's a digital meter, it's probably a kH factor of 1.0, and you can ignore it. Older analog meters often have a kH factor of 7.2, which you'll need to use in your calculation. Use this formula to determine how much energy that appliance uses in an hour:

$$3600 \text{ (sec/hr)} \times \frac{\text{beats counted}}{\text{seconds recorded}} \times \text{kH factor} = \text{kW per hour}$$

Multiply this number by 24 to see how much energy is used by the appliance in a full day of use.

 **MYTH**

DOES KEEPING BATTERIES IN THE FRIDGE REALLY MAKE THEM LAST LONGER?

In a webisode, Grant, Kari, and Tory determined the truth behind the idea that how you store your batteries will impact how long they last. Some people pile up batteries in the fridge because they believe it'll make them last longer. Others warm up batteries with their hands before putting them in a device because that's supposed to extend their life. Do either of these things work, or should you save your time and fridge space?

WHAT YOU'LL NEED:

- ☐ 3 identical battery-operated toys
- ☐ 3 sets of batteries for the toys you've chosen (purchased at the same time and with the same expiration dates) **$$**
- ☐ 1 refrigerator
- ☐ 2 friends (optional)
- ☐ A shirt or pants with a pocket that keeps items close to your body

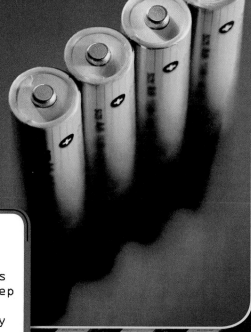

TIME REQUIRED:
Several weeks
to store the
batteries, plus
1-2 days to keep
the batteries
going till they
run down

WHAT TO DO:

STEP 1 Before you begin your experiment, place 1 set of batteries in a safe place in a refrigerator. Leave these batteries for a minimum of 2 weeks.

STEP 2 About a half hour before you're ready to test your batteries, warm up one of the sets that did not go in the refrigerator for at least 30 minutes by placing the batteries in a pocket that is exposed to your body heat, or by holding them in your closed hand.

STEP 3 If you have friends to help you, you can test all 3 sets of batteries at once. Place each set of batteries in a toy, being sure to make a note of which batteries are in which toy, and turn all 3 toys on at once. Keep them running until the batteries die and see which lasts the longest. If you're running the experiment on your own, do 1 toy at a time and use a stopwatch to determine the length of time needed to run down the batteries. Make a note of each trial and compare the times at the end.

WHAT'S YOUR CONCLUSION?

☐ **Confirmed**
☐ **Plausible**
☐ **Busted**

MAKE MODELS OF SUSTAINABLE ENERGY DEVICES.

If you follow the news, you'll notice lots of people claiming they've got ways to collect free energy. With gas and oil prices skyrocketing, these devices could be worth their weight in gold. Unfortunately, Jamie and Adam looked into the most popular devices and determined that this myth was BUSTED. But that doesn't mean that you can't find alternative, sustainable sources of energy that don't rely on fossil fuels. Here are some models you can build to demonstrate the most effective forms of sustainable energy machines in use today.

TRY THIS: BUILD A MODEL SOLAR CELL.

WHAT YOU'LL NEED:

- ☐ 2 pieces of copper sheet, approximately 5 inches square*
- ☐ 1 pair of metal scissors
- ☐ 1 electric stove or hot plate of at least 1000 watts
- ☐ 2 alligator clips
- ☐ Water
- ☐ Salt
- ☐ 1 large bowl
- ☐ 1 set of measuring spoons
- ☐ 1 clear 2-liter plastic bottle cut in half
- ☐ 1 sensitive micro-ammeter that can read 10–50 microamperes*
- ☐ 1 piece of sandpaper or wire brush

They're appearing all over the place: those shiny black panels on top of homes and offices. These are solar cells, and they're designed to collect energy from the sun and store it in batteries. Then those batteries are used to power appliances around houses and office buildings.

*Copper sheets and micro-ammeters can be purchased online or at your local hardware store.

WARNING:

Ask an adult to help you perform this experiment. You should not use the stove or a hot plate by yourself without permission from a parent or teacher.

TIME REQUIRED: 1 hour

Real solar cells are huge, expensive, and use advanced metals and technology, but it's possible to build a simple model of a cell to see how they work. Here's how:

WHAT TO DO:

STEP 1 Cut your copper sheets so they're small enough to just fit onto your stove burner. Wash your hands with soap to remove any dirt and oil, and do the same for your copper sheets. Set 1 sheet aside and ask your adult helper to place the other on a burner set to High.

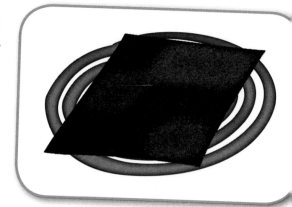

STEP 2 Heat the copper sheet for about 30 minutes. This is going to cause the copper to oxidize, which will make cool colors and patterns appear on the surface of the copper and eventually create a black coating on the outside. This is fun to watch, but do NOT touch the copper — it's incredibly hot.

When the copper has become almost completely black, turn off the burner. Leave the copper where it is until it cools to room temperature. This should take about 20 minutes. As it cools, the black coating should start to shrink and peel off.

STEP 3 When the copper sheet is cool, run it under water and gently remove as much of the black coating as possible. You may use your sandpaper or metal brush to help the process, but be gentle. You want to keep the colorful layer that's just beneath the black oxide, and if you scrub the sheet too much you'll remove it.

STEP 4 Take the bottom half of your 2-liter bottle and the 2 copper sheets — the one that you oxidized and the one that you set aside. Curve the sheets so they lie along the inside of the bottle with the side of the copper that touched the stove facing into the middle. Without the sheets touching (trim them if you need to), hold them in place from the top of the bottle with the alligator clips, 1 on each sheet.

STEP 5 In a separate bowl or jar, mix 3 tablespoons of salt with 3 cups of warm water. Stir them until the salt is dissolved, and then add this solution to the bottom of the 2-liter bottle. You want at least an inch of the sheets sticking out above the water in case you need to adjust it — and so that the alligator clips stay dry.

STEP 6 Connect the leads of the alligator clips to the micro-ammeter. The clean sheet should be connected to the positive terminal and the sheet you heated should connect to the negative terminal. Your meter may detect a small electric current at this point.

STEP 7 Place your solar cell in bright sunlight and observe the micro-ammeter. How much current is produced? Try blocking the sunlight and seeing how the energy production is impacted.

What Happened?

Sunlight causes electrons in the copper oxide, something we call a semi-conductor, to gain energy and break loose from the metal. This allows them to flow through the salt water to the clean copper plate and through the circuit, which generates electricity. Powering a 100-watt light bulb with a cell like this would need a sheet of copper oxide with an area of about 80 square meters, which would be expensive and tricky to find a place for in your house. The solar cells people actually use are built on the same basic principle, but with more efficient metals and high-tech interactions that create more energy from a smaller cell.

TRY THIS: MAKE A BIOGAS DIGESTER.

Alternative sources of fuel can be things that generate electricity, like wind, but also substances that can be burned in place of coal or oil. One gas used for burning is methane, which can be produced naturally by living organisms. The most important producer of methane is bacteria that are found in many places, including the intestines of cows.

When the bacteria digest their food, which can be undigested food of cows (or other animals), they take the energy out of the food for themselves and produce methane gas. If you contain the bacteria while they eat, you can capture the methane and use it for fuel. That's what we're going to try in this next experiment.

WARNING:

The gas you will produce in this experiment is flammable. You won't produce enough of it to be very dangerous, but you should still keep your digester away from flames or sparks. Use gloves and goggles when working with cow dung.

TIME REQUIRED: 60 minutes to set up, several weeks for digestion and gas formation

WHAT YOU'LL NEED:

- ☐ 1 2-liter bottle
- ☐ Distilled water
- ☐ 1 pair of scissors
- ☐ 3 sturdy drinking straws, 4-6 inches long, bent into an L. These should fit snugly into the hole of the stopper.
- ☐ 2 pieces of rubber tubing, each about 1 foot long
- ☐ 1 1-hole stopper that fits in the top of the 2-liter bottle*
- ☐ Dead organic matter like dead leaves, grass cuttings, or vegetable table scraps
- ☐ Bacteria source — natural soil or fresh cow dung
- ☐ 1 bucket, large pot, or small trash can
- ☐ 1 funnel-shaped Mylar balloon
- ☐ 1 gardening spade
- ☐ 2 clamps or clothespins
- ☐ Black paper
- ☐ 1 pair of rubber gloves
- ☐ 1 pair of goggles

*Be sure to use a lubricant like glycerin on your straw when you push it into a stopper, or you'll risk breaking the straw. If you don't have access to rubber or cork stoppers with holes, you can secure the straw in place in the bottle using duct tape.

WHAT TO DO:

STEP 1 First, you'll make your gas digester. Pour distilled water into the 2-liter bottle until it's ⅔ full. Then pour water from the bottle into the bucket. Add 1 or 2 cups of dead organic matter or table scraps and ½ cup of soil or cow manure. Cow manure works best, but soil is fine, too. Use the spade to mix these together until any chunks are broken up. Then use the funnel to pour this mixture back into the bottle. Leave several inches at the top of the bottle empty.

STEP 2 Cover the outside of the bottle with black paper. This will keep out light and prevent algae from growing, which can slow the production of gas.

STEP 3 Using the 1-hole stopper, place the straw into the top of the bottle. The tubing needs to be at least an inch above the mixture. If you're using duct tape, wrap the tape around the straw or tubing and close the top of the bottle so that there are no air leaks. Be careful not to compress the straw; this will close the passage for the gas leaving the bottle.

STEP 4 Connect a piece of rubber tubing to the straw. Place another straw in the open end of this rubber tubing and then connect the second piece of rubber tubing to the second straw.

Place the third straw on the end of the second piece of rubber and insert this tube into the opening of a deflated Mylar balloon. Use the duct tape to seal all the connections so that no gas can leak between the bottle and the balloon. You'll want to be able to remove the second piece of rubber tubing in order to test the gas

collected in the balloon, so make sure to tape it accordingly. Finally, take care that none of the straws are squashed or crushed, as this will prevent the gas from traveling to the balloon.

STEP 5 Place your digester somewhere warm where it can sit for 3 to 6 weeks. Make sure it isn't near any open flames or sparks. You'll be able to see gas collecting as the balloon inflates. The first gas to leave the digester will be carbon dioxide, which isn't flammable, so when the balloon becomes slightly inflated, close the first rubber tube with a clamp or clothespin.

This will keep gas from escaping the digester. Then detach the second rubber tube. Flatten the balloon to push all the gas you collected out. This will ensure that the gas you test will have a higher percentage of methane, making it more flammable.

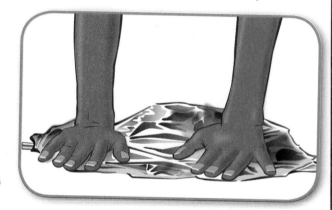

STEP 6 Reattach the balloon, making sure there are no leaks, and unclamp the rubber tubing. Let the digester sit until the balloon has inflated.

STEP 7 ▶ Ask your science teacher if he or she can help you test the flammability of this gas. DO NOT try to test the gas yourself. You can bring the gas to school by clamping both rubber tubes and detaching the second tube with the balloon still attached. We recommend testing the gas by filling a small container, like a test tube, with water; inverting it in another container of water (without spilling any water out of the test tube); and then displacing the water in the test tube with the gas you collected. You can do this by placing the tube from the balloon under water and into the

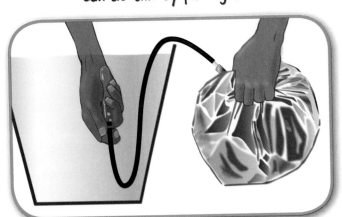

open mouth of the inverted test tube. Put pressure on the balloon to push the gas out of the tube, and it will rise into the test tube and push the water out. When all of the water is out of the test tube, you can lift it straight up and cork it, keeping the gas trapped inside.

Methane is lighter than air, so as long as the test tube is upside down it will stay in the container. Be careful not to put the jar of gas anywhere near a flame or spark until you are ready to test the gas. When you're ready, bring a lit match near the mouth of the test tube and open it. Immediately put the match right at the opening (but not inside the test tube). The gas should cause a burst in the flame and a loud POP as it rises out of the test tube.

If your gas didn't ignite, try filling the test tube again. If it still doesn't work, your sample may have too much carbon dioxide in it. Collect more gas and try again.

 **DO PIRATE EYE PATCHES IMPROVE NIGHT VISION?**

Whether he's protecting his ship from attack or bringing goods above or below deck, a pirate's work is never done. From the bright light of a ship deck to the darkness in the hull, when something needs to happen, a pirate can't wait for his eyes to adjust. But if 1 eye is always ready to be plunged into darkness, then a pirate is ready for anything. *Arrrrr* you ready to try this one, matey?

 TIME REQUIRED: 45 minutes

WHAT YOU'LL NEED:

- ☐ 1 good-quality eye patch
- ☐ 1 eye exam chart or a room set up with an obstacle course or treasure hunt
- ☐ 2–3 test subjects

WHAT TO DO:

STEP 1 Decide how you'll test your subjects. You can either use the eye exam chart — you can make your own or print one out from the internet — or you can create an obstacle course or treasure hunt in a dark room. You might place a number of objects in a dark room for your test subject to find his way around, or you can place a specific object, like a stuffed animal, in a dark room and tell the person to find it. Just be careful your test subject doesn't trip and hurt himself. Make objects large and at least waist-high (like a chair).

STEP 2 Test your subjects by putting the eye patch over 1 eye. Have each person go from a brightly lit space to the dark room where the test will take place. If you're using an eye chart, see how close the person has to move to the chart to read it, or set a specific distance from the chart and see how long it takes his or her eyes to adjust till the letters become visible. If you're using an obstacle course or treasure hunt, time the person to see how long it takes him or her to complete the test.

T E 10 $\frac{20}{100}$

P V L 7 $\frac{20}{70}$

H C O E 5 $\frac{20}{50}$

H P D N L 4 $\frac{20}{40}$

D V H T L U 3 $\frac{20}{30}$

E V O U C T Y 2 $\frac{20}{25}$

P C Y L H N D V 1 $\frac{20}{20}$

STEP 3 ▶ Have your test subjects wear the eye patch over 1 eye for at least 30 minutes. Just before entering the darkened room, have the person switch the eye patch to the other eye. Let the person enter the darkened room and repeat the first test. If you're doing a treasure hunt, you may want to place the object in a different place this time. Compare the length of time it takes your subject to complete the test to the results with the eye that hadn't been covered with a patch. If you used the eye exam chart, compare the distances at which the person was able to read the chart or the time it took his eyes to adjust enough to read the chart.

Did covering the eye make it darkness-ready, or was this myth as phony as buried pirate treasure?

WHAT'S YOUR CONCLUSION?

☐ **Confirmed**
☐ **Plausible**
☐ **Busted**

What Happened?

Our eyes work with 2 types of cells. Cones are cells that are sensitive to light, and rods are cells that work better in the dark. For rods to work they need to warm up, which requires 25–30 minutes of being in the dark. By keeping one eye in the dark with a patch, the rods are warmed up and ready to go when you're plunged into darkness. So when you need to race to the deck to fire cannons at other ships, you can remove the patch and see well right away with that eye — you don't have to wait for the rods to start working.

MYTH

CAN A SNEEZE REALLY TRAVEL UP TO 30 FEET?

It seems like every year there are new warnings about how fast and far germs can travel. The MythBusters have taken on a bunch of these icky ideas, and now you can, too. If you happen to have a cold, testing these out will be a fantastic way to make yourself feel better about feeling so bad.

WHAT YOU'LL NEED:

☐ 30 feet of white paper
☐ 1 tape measure
☐ 1 marker
☐ 1 package of food coloring*
☐ Water

*Be sure to wear clothes and work in a place that can be stained with food coloring.

TIME REQUIRED:
20 minutes and up

WHAT TO DO:

STEP 1 Lay out a strip of test paper. You can use a long table or line of desks, like Jamie and Adam did, or just lay the paper down on the ground. Use your tape measure to mark out distance on the paper from 0–30 feet. Mark at least each foot, and use smaller increments if you'd like more precise measurements.

STEP 2 Decide who's going to be sneezing. If you watched the show, you'll know that making someone sneeze on cue can be really tricky. If you want, you can experiment with putting a little ground red, white, or black pepper on your fingertip and rubbing it at the base of your nostrils. The problem is that this can cause skin irritation and make your nose uncomfortable whether you sneeze or not. We recommend you do this experiment during allergy season and find someone who's already sneezing a lot to help you out. This way you make use of a person who's already miserable, rather than making a new person miserable to help you.

STEP 3 Get the sneezing person to stand at the base of your sneeze paper at the 0 distance marker. Have the person take a swig of food coloring or water with a lot of food coloring in it and face the white paper strip. Now you just have to wait for it . . .

Wait for it. . . .

Wait for it. . . .

ACHOO!

Once your person sneezes, see how far the color splattered down the paper. Did it make it all the way to 30 feet?

WHAT'S YOUR CONCLUSION?

☐ **Confirmed**

☐ **Plausible**

☐ **Busted**

TRY THIS:

Have different friends drink different colors of food coloring and see how each one compares to the other. Do one person's sneezes travel farther than another?

MYTH

FLU FICTION #2

WHAT'S THE BEST WAY TO STOP A SNEEZE?

Now that you've got someone sneezing colorful sneezes, the next myth is easy to test. If you want to stop the spread of germs, where should you direct that sneeze? Into your hands? Into a tissue? Into your elbow? Keep your sneezer sneezing and find out.

TIME REQUIRED:
20 minutes

WHAT YOU'LL NEED:
- ☐ 1 sneezing person
- ☐ 1 package of food coloring
- ☐ White paper with distance markings
- ☐ 1 tissue or handkerchief
- ☐ Old clothes that can be stained
- ☐ 1 glass of water for rinsing sneeze stain

$

WHAT TO DO:

STEP 1   If you're using the same white paper you used to test the last myth, make sure you switch to a new color of food coloring for sneeze staining. If you used several colors on the first sheet, you'll probably want to start with a clean sheet. Set out about 10 feet of white paper and mark off each foot using a tape measure.

STEP 2 — Have your sneezer take a mouthful of food coloring and face the paper. The first time he or she sneezes, have him or her cover his or her mouth with his or her hands. See how far onto the paper any spray traveled, if at all. Repeat this technique a few times.

STEP 3 — To test the next technique, rinse the sneezer's mouth with several mouthfuls of water before taking a swig of a new color. It's best to use light colors first and graduate to a darker color for each trial. When the person sneezes this time, have him or her cover his or her mouth and nose with the handkerchief. See how far the sneeze spray traveled. Repeat this technique a few times.

STEP 4 — Repeat the rinsing and re-staining as you did in step 2, using your darkest color stain. When the person sneezes, have him or her cover her mouth with his or her elbow and make note of how far the sneeze spray traveled. Repeat this technique a few times.

STEP 5 — Compare the distances the sneeze spray traveled in each situation. Did one technique block the sneeze most effectively? If so, tell everyone you know — now you know the best way to keep sneeze germs contained!

MYTH

FLU FICTION #3

DOES A RUNNY NOSE REALLY RUN ALL OVER THE PLACE?

Could nasal secretions really travel so far so fast it would be almost impossible not to come into contact with them? If you know someone with a cold, this may be a good time to uncover the truth about her far-flung snot.

WHAT YOU'LL NEED:

☐ Fluorescent liquid*
☐ 1/4 cup measuring cup
☐ 1 black light
☐ An activity to keep you busy, like building a model or playing solitaire

TIME REQUIRED:
An hour and a half

*The fluorescent liquid is our stand-in for snot. This includes fluid you can purchase specifically for lighting under a black light or things at home that you may have access to. Liquid laundry detergent usually works.

WHAT TO DO:

STEP 1 ▶ If you've got a bad cold and a runny nose, you can actually use your own snot for this experiment. Yes, it's gross but true — your snot will glow under a black light. Just make sure your nose is running enough that you can wipe it regularly with your hand.

If you don't have a cold, you'll need to use fake snot. This is where the fluorescent liquid comes in handy. Adam and Jamie discovered that a person's nose can secrete snot at a rate of 60 milliliters per hour. That's a quarter cup of snot every 60 minutes! Measure out a quarter cup of laundry detergent and keep it near you for the next hour.

STEP 2 ▶ Figure out how you'll spend the hour for your test. You'll want to do something in a room that can get dirty, and that can be made dark to shine your black light on. A garage or basement are good options. Make sure you're wearing clothes that can get dirty, too.

If you have some friends who can come over to play a game of cards or work on a project together, that would be ideal. Another option is to start a project like building a model or working on a puzzle. Set up your working space, have your snot cup close at hand, and start the clock.

STEP 3 If your nose were running at a rate of 60 milliliters an hour, you'd be wiping it several times a minute. About every 10 or 15 seconds, touch your fingers to your snot stand-in. Try doing this with the side of your finger or back of your hand, the place you'd touch if you were wiping your nose — that will get you the most realistic results.

Keep this up for an hour, touching your snot and behaving the way you would if you'd been wiping your nose (maybe wiping it on your clothes, maybe not . . .).

STEP 4 At the end of the hour, turn off the lights and turn on your black light. Shine the light around the room and all over yourself and your friends. Where do you see snot illuminated? Did it travel as far as the myth says? If you were spreading snot this fast, would a healthy person stand a chance in the same room as you?

WHAT'S YOUR CONCLUSION?
- ☐ **Confirmed**
- ☐ **Plausible**
- ☐ **Busted**

CAN YOU REALLY CATCH SOMEONE'S COLD JUST BY SHAKING HANDS?

It's a lot of fun being a MythBuster. Not only do you get to do all kinds of crazy experiments, but you meet lots of interesting people, too. Of course, that means shaking lots of hands and, during cold season, picking up a lot of germs. In a popular webisode, Jamie and Adam tried to determine just how many germs Jamie would pick up on a standard day of pressing palms, but they seemed to have a sampling error, and their results were inconclusive. Now you can try the experiment and see if you can get better results than the professionals!

WHAT YOU'LL NEED:

- [ ] 1 pack of cotton swabs
- [ ] 4 petri dishes
- [ ] Nutrient agar*
- [ ] 1 roll of masking tape
- [ ] 1 marker
- [ ] A warm place
- [ ] 1 digital thermometer

TIME REQUIRED:
30 minutes for making agar plates; 2 hours for plates to set; an hour for contaminating your hand; 3 days to incubate; 20 minutes to make observations and clean up.

*Petri dishes and nutrient agar can be purchased from online suppliers or stores that supply materials for science experiments. Make sure you purchase nutrient agar that isn't prepared to grow specific microbes. Look for plain nutrient agar or LB agar. You can purchase ready-made agar plates (agar pre-poured in petri dishes), or you can purchase dishes and the materials needed to make the agar.

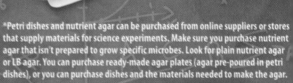

MAKE YOUR OWN AGAR

If you are not able to purchase nutrient agar and plates, use the following procedure and ask an adult to help you make your own:

WHAT YO
- ☐ 2 packets o
- ☐ 4 teaspoon
- ☐ Saucepan
- ☐ 2 cups of water
- ☐ 2 cubes of beef bullion
- ☐ Petri dishes or muffin tins and foil liners
- ☐ Measuring spoons
- ☐ Sealable plastic baggies

1. In the saucepan, combine water with the gelatin packets, sugar, and bullion cubes. This should be enough for around 10–15 plates.

2. Bring this mixture to a boil. Be sure to stir it constantly while it's heating. After it has boiled, turn off the heat.

3. Let this mixture cool slightly, for about 10 minutes (not so much that it starts to set), then pour it into your dishes so they are 1/3 to 1/2 full. If you are using a muffin pan and liners, place the liners into the pan and then pour your gelatin mixture.

4. Let the dishes cool until the gelatin has set. If you have access to a refrigerator, placing the gelatin, uncovered, in the fridge to cool is ideal.

5. If you are using muffin cups, once the gel has set, carefully remove the molds from the liners and place them into plastic baggies, one gel per baggie. Be careful not to touch the gels. If you are using petri dishes, once the gels are cooled place a lid on each. Keep your plates or baggies refrigerated until you are ready to use them. Use them within 3 days.

WHAT TO DO:

Your first set of petri dishes will grow samples collected from a hand that hasn't been shaken by lots of people. You want this hand to be reasonably clean, but not within minutes of being washed. If you've washed your hand in the last hour or so and not been in contact with a lot of people, you should be ready to go.

Use your cotton swab and rub the underside of your right hand several times. Without touching the swab to anything else, rub the cotton across the surface of one of your petri dishes and close the lid (or place the gelatin in its plastic baggie). Use your marker and tape to label this sample HAND, BOTTOM, 1. Repeat this process with a clean swab for the top of your right hand and label the container HAND, TOP, 1.

STEP 2 Decide how you will find 40 different people to shake hands with. Maybe you can find people at the playground or at school. You can include people in your family and friends. Keep track of how many hands you've shaken, and when you reach 40, stop shaking hands. Don't touch anything else with this hand until you've collected your sample.

Using a clean cotton swab each time, repeat step 1 now that your hand has been exposed. Label the samples HAND, BOTTOM, 2 and HAND, TOP, 2.

STEP 3 ▶ Once all your petri dishes are labeled, use your tape to seal the container. Put them in a warm place to sit for 48 hours. You might decide to place the dishes under a warm lamp or near a heater. Place a thermometer in the location you choose and try to keep the temperature as close to 90 degrees Fahrenheit as you can.

STEP 4 ▶ After 48 hours, observe your samples. Has anything changed? Most bacteria should have started to grow by now, and would resemble a smudge or spots on the surface of the gel. Give the samples 24 more hours to sit.

STEP 5 ▶ After a total of 72 hours of incubation, make your final observations. Do you see any differences? Count the number of colonies on the HAND 1 and HAND 2 dishes and compare them. Are there more on the second set of dishes? Or, like Jamie and Adam, did you find different types of growth on the dishes? When you're finished making observations, wrap your samples in newspaper and throw them in the trash without opening them (none of us need exposure to more germs!).

WHAT'S YOUR CONCLUSION?

☐ **Confirmed**
☐ **Plausible**
☐ **Busted**

Did You Know?

A lot of what grows on petri dishes like this isn't bacteria or germs at all — it's fungus! A fungus is something like a mushroom or mold that grows from spores that are released into the environment. There are millions of fungal spores in the air all around us, just waiting for the right conditions to start growing. If all the fungal spores in the world started growing at once, the entire surface of the Earth would be buried in fungus.

TRY THIS: TEST THE EFFECT OF SANITIZERS ON BACTERIA AND FUNGAL GROWTH.

WHAT YOU'LL NEED:

- ☐ 1 pack of cotton swabs
- ☐ 8 petri dishes
- ☐ Nutrient agar
- ☐ Antibacterial solutions such as hand sanitizer; antibacterial hand or dish soap; disinfectant air spray; antibacterial cleaning solution
- ☐ 1 roll of masking tape
- ☐ 1 marker
- ☐ A warm place
- ☐ 1 digital thermometer

These days it seems like everything around us is antibacterial: hand soap, dish soap, hand sanitizers, counter cleaners. But do any of these products make a difference, or are they just a waste of money and time?

TIME REQUIRED: 30 minutes for making agar plates; 2 hours for plates to set; 20 minutes to prepare samples; 3 days to incubate; 20 minutes to make observations and clean up.

WHAT TO DO:

STEP 1 ▶ Prepare at least 8 agar gels, or use ones left from the last experiment.

STEP 2 ▶ Collect samples off of your hand, front and back, with a clean cotton swab, and swipe the swab onto all your agar plates. Label the plates and seal them with tape.

STEP 3 ▶ Prepare plates to match each of your initial samples by treating the gels with your choice of antibacterial substance. Try at least 2 or 3 different ones for all of your initial samples so you can compare their effectiveness. Apply the antibacterials to the gels by dampening a paper towel with them and swiping the towel across the surface of the gel. You want to make sure the substance is applied, but you don't want the surface of the gel to become wet, as this may degrade it. Make sure you label your gels so you know which substance is on which sample.

STEP 4 ▶ When the gels are treated, repeat Step 2 for your hands and each of the dishes with an antibacterial. When you are finished, you should have sets with labels like this: HAND, BOTTOM, ANTIBACTERIAL SOAP and HAND, BOTTOM, HAND SANITIZER.

STEP 5 ▶ Seal your second set of samples and place them in a warm, safe place. Try to monitor the temperature and keep the samples as close to 90 degrees as possible.

After 48 hours, observe your samples. Observe them again after 72 hours. Did the antibacterial substances prevent things from growing, or did just as much grow whether the plates were treated or not? Which substances were most effective at preventing growth?

TRY THIS: DETECT AND COLLECT LATENT FINGERPRINTS.

Jamie and Adam tried to fool Grant's fingerprint-scanner lock by creating a fake version of his print. You might have noticed that the team *intentionally* left out a critical step in this process so people at home can't actually break into other people's locks. But we *can* tell you how to dust and lift latent prints, just like they did in this episode. What you do with the prints once you've lifted them is up to you.

WHAT YOU'LL NEED:

- ☐ Talcum powder, baby powder, or other light/white powder
- ☐ Printer toner or finely powdered charcoal
- ☐ A fine brush with soft bristles (a paintbrush or clean makeup brush will work)
- ☐ 2 small dishes
- ☐ Wide transparent tape, such as packing tape
- ☐ Black and white cards, such as index cards
- ☐ Strong light source, such as a bright desk lamp
- ☐ 1 black light (optional)
- ☐ Gloves

TIME REQUIRED:
15 minutes and up

WHAT TO DO:

STEP 1

First, you'll need to practice dusting for prints. This will be easiest if you create prints as carefully as possible on a clean item like a drinking glass. Wearing your gloves, choose your item (a glass, mirror, or computer screen work nicely), wipe the surface clean with a rag, and then carefully press one of your fingers onto the object in several places. Be careful to place and lift your finger without smearing the print. This will work best if your hands haven't been washed recently, or if you've recently used moisturizer.

Once you've placed your print, use your bright light to illuminate the object. Make a note of the appearance of the print under the light. If you're using a black light, repeat this step with your black light.

STEP 2

Next, pour a small amount of your light powder and your dark powder into the two dishes. Using the brush, lightly dip the tip into one of the powders and apply it to a print (or the area where you expect there to be a print) by making very gentle, circular motions. You barely want to touch the print with the brush — just enough that a few grains of powder at a time will stick to the print.

Continue dipping your brush into the powder and circling it over the area until the print becomes visible. Try to follow the ridges of the print, and stop as soon as the full print is revealed. Use the other powder on a different one. See if one works better than the other. Gently blow away excess powder.

STEP 3 ▶ Dusting the prints is the hardest part, but lifting the prints takes some skill, too. Unroll a few inches of your clear tape and hold it over the powdered prints you plan to lift. Begin pressing the tape onto the object 1-2 inches before your print starts and continue pressing it for at least an inch after the print. Use different pieces of tape for prints dusted with light and dark powder, and be careful to press the tape down smoothly without any air bubbles forming.

STEP 4 ▶ Once the tape is covering the print, carefully peel the strip away, being sure not to let the tape fold over and stick to itself anywhere. Choose a card with a color that contrasts the powder you used to dust the print and carefully lay the tape onto it, again being careful to prevent air bubbles. Cut the tape from the roll and trim it so it isn't extending beyond the edges of the card. Now you have the print in evidence!

Practice lifting prints off different objects as many times as necessary to feel confident about the process. You can even try smearing a print intentionally to see what kind of result that produces.

Once you've got the technique down, try testing different objects you come across. You might use a glass someone left out after they used it, a doorknob, the handle of a car . . . anywhere there's a smooth surface where someone may have pressed his or her fingertips. Use the next experiment to see if you can determine whose mitts left behind the prints you discover.

TRY THIS: COLLECT AND COMPARE FINGERPRINT DATA.

WHAT YOU'LL NEED:

☐ White paper
☐ 1 pen or pencil
☐ 1 inkpad
☐ Willing test subjects

TIME REQUIRED:
5 minutes and up

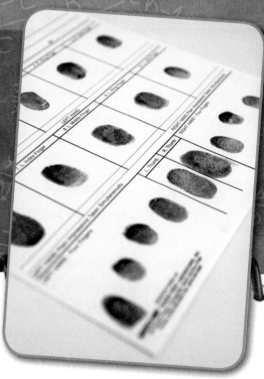

WHAT TO DO:

STEP 1 ▷ Find out who your suspects are. You might collect the prints of people who live in your home, or simply collect prints from willing passersby (in which case you should prepare several blank print forms ahead of time and leave a space for the person's name). For each subject, set up a fingerprint form by labeling the top of the paper with the person's name and dividing the remaining space into 2 sections. Label the first section RIGHT HAND and the other section LEFT HAND. Then draw boxes, about 2 inches on a side, and label each box with a finger (THUMB, INDEX, MIDDLE, RING, PINKY). Place the fingers of one hand so they match the corresponding finger of the opposite hand.

STEP 2 Now that your sheets are set up, it's time to fill in your database of fingerprints. For each person whose prints you collect, be sure the print form is labeled with his or her name. Have the person press 1 finger at a time onto the inkpad, and then press a print into the appropriate box on the form. The print should be made by firmly rolling the fingertip from left to right, and then carefully lifting the finger away. Make sure you get all 10 prints in the appropriate boxes.

STEP 3 You have 2 options for how to use the fingerprints you've collected. The first is simply to use your data to show that none of your subjects have matching prints. Each person's prints will be unique from all the others you collect and will be further identifiable through scars. You can create a display that shows just how different people's prints are. If you have access to a copy machine, you can even blow up some of the prints to make this more obvious.

The second option is to use this set of data to try to match prints you collected in the last experiment. If you collected the prints of everyone in your house, can you match an unknown print that you collected earlier? First try to narrow down what finger the latent print you lifted was made by: Is it bigger? It may be a thumb. Smaller? Possibly a pinky. Then compare the card with the lifted print to the print forms that correspond to known people. Now you may be able to prove exactly who's been leaving their dirty dishes for someone else to pick up!

MYTH

IS IT TRUE THAT PEOPLE CAN'T WALK IN A STRAIGHT LINE?

If you saw the show, then you know the answer to this one. But that doesn't mean you can't have some fun, *MythBusters*-style. See how well you can do with these challenges, and then you can see if your friends can do better. The best part? This experiment is as easy as walking down the street.

WHAT YOU'LL NEED:

- ☐ I blindfold
- ☐ I pair of noise-canceling headphones*
- ☐ I bucket that fits over your head
- ☐ I or more partners
- ☐ An open space

TIME REQUIRED:
One hour

*These can be pricy to buy new, but you can find used sets available for as low as $30 if you search online.

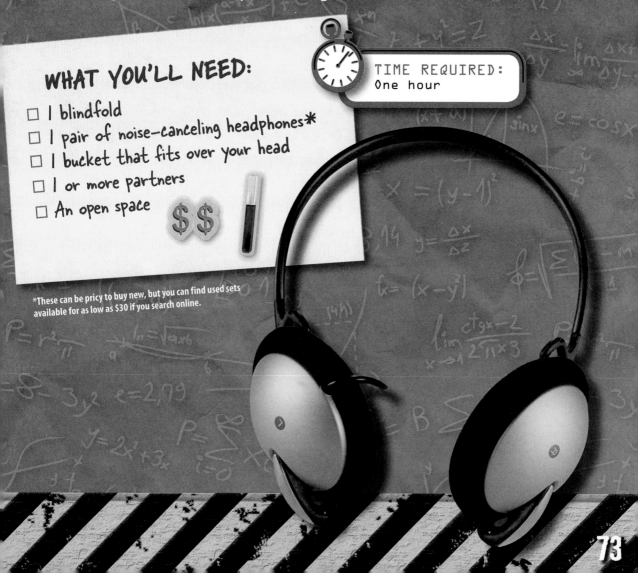

WHAT TO DO: Part 1

STEP 1 The first part of this experiment is to see if a person can walk in a straight line without the aid of eyes and ears. Find a safe, open space like a large lawn or athletic field. An athletic field is ideal because you can use the lines of the field for your straight line.

STEP 2 Set out the straight line for walking. This could be along the sidelines of an athletic field or directly toward another person who can be standing at a distance of 50 yards (half a football field) from the person who will be walking.

STEP 3 Place the blindfold and headphones on the person walking. This is to prevent the person from having the benefit of light and sounds to help determine a direction. Once their vision and hearing are cut off, have him or her start walking. See how long it takes him or her to get off course, and how far off course different people get. Is one person better at walking straight than others, or is everyone equally bad at this? Did anyone manage to walk in a straight line?

WHAT'S YOUR CONCLUSION?

- ☐ **Confirmed**
- ☐ **Plausible**
- ☐ **Busted**

Part 2

Now you can repeat the second part of this experiment, which determines how well a person can navigate with extremely limited vision. You'll show what it would be like for someone who couldn't see more than a small space around himself in a severe rain or snowstorm. In fact, placing a bucket on one's head and finding one's way is a time-honored way of training people to navigate white-out snow conditions. Like Jamie and Adam say, sometimes the simplest technique is the best.

STEP 1 ▶ Find a place to navigate. This will work best if there are some things for the person to find his or her way around, like a playground or forest. Find a starting place and determine a finishing spot that is in a straight line about 50 yards away.

STEP 2 ▶ Place the bucket on the person's head and send him or her on his or her way. How well do the people you test do? Do the more experienced hikers have more success than other people, or does everyone wind up way off course when they can't use their eyes to get around obstacles?

Did You Know?

Being able to find your way in the woods without the aid of visual cues is something orienteers train for. Adam was lost almost from the start, while Jamie succeeded because he kept track of every turn and step he made to avoid obstacles. That's how Jamie was always able to get back to his original path while Adam just stumbled around. But Adam learned something, too—who to take as a partner the next time he goes hiking in the woods!

DOES A BASEBALL BAT REALLY HAVE A SWEET SPOT?

The MythBusters have tested a bunch of baseball myths — eye black, sliding into bases, hitting the hide off a ball — but what about whether or not a baseball bat has a sweet spot? You know the sweet spot — that exact place on the bat that, if you hit the ball with it, gives your hit some extra oomph when you swing for the fences. Here's how to investigate this one for yourself. Who knows, maybe it'll be your ticket to the big leagues!

WHAT YOU'LL NEED:

- ☐ 1 wooden baseball bat
- ☐ 1 hammer
- ☐ 1 roll of masking tape
- ☐ 1 baseball or softball
- ☐ A partner

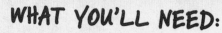

WHAT TO DO:

STEP 1 ▶ Hold the bat at the base like you're going to swing it, and have your partner start using the hammer to hit the bat. Your partner should start at the tip and move down the bat a little at a time. Make sure the bat isn't touching the ground while you do this.

TIME REQUIRED
15 minutes

STEP 2 ▶ You'll feel the vibrations in the bat each time the hammer hits it. As your partner moves the hammer along the bat, he or she will eventually come to a place where you no longer feel vibrations when he or she hits the bat. Double-check this spot a few times to be sure you've got the right one, and then mark it with your masking tape.

STEP 3 ▶ Now your partner needs to do some pitching. Your goal is to hit the ball with the bat in the exact place you put your tape. When you hit the right spot, what effect does it have on your power? If you're interested, you could check an aluminum bat to see if it has a sweet spot, too.

What do you think? Is the sweet spot the secret to the success of today's heavy hitters?

WHAT'S YOUR CONCLUSION?

- ☐ **Confirmed**
- ☐ **Plausible**
- ☐ **Busted**

What Happened?

When you hit most places on a bat, the wood vibrates, and you can feel it in your hands. These vibrations are energy moving away from the ball, which means it's energy that's NOT propelling the ball forward. When you hit the sweet spot, the lack of vibrations means all the energy was transferred back into the ball, making it go farther faster.

TRY THIS: BUILD A DUCT-TAPE HAMMOCK.

Duct tape — that magic material that makes so many things possible. A duct-tape boat? Sure. A duct-tape cannon? No problem. Lifting a 5,000-pound car? Piece of cake. So it should be no surprise that duct tape can hold your weight easily . . . and comfortably! Here's how to build a duct-tape hammock that will amaze your friends and family. The hardest part is finding a place to hang it.

WHAT YOU'LL NEED:

- ☐ 3 rolls of duct tape
- ☐ 1 pair of scissors
- ☐ 2 wooden dowels (4 feet long, 1 inch thick)
- ☐ 5 or 6 feet of strong rope
- ☐ 1 ruler
- ☐ 1 marker
- ☐ 1 broomstick (or other strong pole longer than 3 feet and at least 1 inch thick)

TIME REQUIRED:
1-2 hours

WHAT TO DO:

STEP 1 The dowels are going to act as the ends of your hammock. The duct tape will be attached to them as you form strips that run the length of your hammock. In order to weave your hammock without the tape sticking to itself and making a mess of things, you'll need to secure the dowels while you work. You can have friends hold the dowels at the desired distance (we suggest between 7 and 8 feet), or you can use clamps to hold them on a table or workspace. It's also possible to anchor them to the ground using a cinder block or other heavy object.

STEP 2 Starting about 6 inches from the edge of the dowel, with the sticky side facing up, pull about a foot of duct tape beyond the wood and start unrolling the tape toward the other dowel. Fold the foot of tape over itself (and around the dowel) to secure the end of the tape. Roll the tape down to the other dowel, around it, and back to the first dowel. Carefully press the 2 sticky sides of tape together as you retrace the first length of tape to make 1 strip with no sticky sides exposed. When you reach the first dowel, cut the tape and press the end down. The side facing up will be the bottom of your hammock.

STEP 3 Starting from the other dowel, repeat this step for the next strip. By alternating ends and changing the length of the strips you fold over to secure them, you'll avoid creating a bump across the hammock that could be uncomfortable when you use it.

STEP 4 Continue making strips until you have covered all but the last 6 inches of wood. You should have 6 inches of wood on both sides when you finish, and about 18 long strips going across. Make sure the strips line up perfectly so no adhesive is exposed and that the strips move independently of each other.

STEP 5 Use your ruler to mark the positions of your horizontal strips on both sides of the hammock. Start from one dowel and measure 7 or 8 inches from the end on the outermost strip of tape. Make a mark with your marker. Continue marking the outermost strip at 7- or 8-inch intervals and make corresponding marks on the outer strip on the other side of the hammock.

STEP 6 You're going to use the broomstick to hold open the long strips so you can weave in horizontal ones. Starting at one end of the hammock, lift the first strip and thread the broomstick under it. Moving across the hammock, thread the broomstick under every other strip and push it a few inches past the mark for your first cross-strip. You'll want to leave about 3 inches between each horizontal strip you add.

STEP 7 Attach the end of a new piece of duct tape to your ruler by pressing the ruler on top of it with the adhesive side facing up. This will allow you to push the ruler through and pull the tape behind it, which will make you less likely to have the tape stick where you don't want it to. Hold the roll of tape on one side and push the strip through with the adhesive side facing up. When you've threaded the tape under the lifted strips (it will run over the other half of them) and reached the other side, make sure your tape is lined up so it lies below your mark. Then fold about 6 inches of tape over on itself to secure the strip. Bring the roll of tape across the top of the hammock to finish the strip, making sure to line the sticky sides up as well as you can, and press them firmly together. Cut the end of the tape when the strip is finished and press the end down. Depending on the number of long strips, you have you may or may not loop under the last strip. Either way is fine.

STEP 8 Slide the broomstick down until it's a few inches past the third markers (skip the second) and repeat step 7. Continue laying down every other strip in this way. You may or may not loop your horizontal strip under the last long strip.

STEP 9 When you reach the end, remove the broomstick and go back to the second set of marks (about 15 inches from the end of the hammock where you started). Thread the broomstick under the second long strip and every other strip from there until you reach the other side of the hammock. Make a new strip following the same instructions from step 7. This set of horizontal strips will not attach to the outer strip, but to the second strip in.

STEP 10 Go to the remaining markers and repeat steps 8 and 9 until all of your horizontal strips have been laid down.

STEP 11 Take about 5 or 6 feet of rope and tie one end to a dowel just past the duct tape. Tie the other side to the opposite end of the dowel. Wrap duct tape around the tied ends of rope to secure them, and then repeat this with another piece of rope and the other dowel.

STEP 12 Find somewhere to hang your hammock and enjoy the fruits of your labor!

CAN SALSA REALLY EAT THROUGH THE BARS OF A JAIL CELL?

If you had 6 years and an endless supply of salsa, would it be enough to break out of prison? That's what this myth claims. The combination of acid and salt in the salsa supposedly ate away the bars of the jail cell, and the culprit broke loose. You may not be willing to wait 6 years to find out the truth, but if you're patient, you can discover the truth in no longer than a few months.

TIME REQUIRED:
Minutes to set up and refresh periodically; 2 to 3 months to let sit.

WHAT YOU'LL NEED:

☐ 2-3 jars of salsa — you can try several types

☐ 2-3 steel bars (at least 6 inches long and ½ to 1 inch thick)

☐ Bowls or jars to hold each steel bar

☐ Optional:
   6-volt battery,
   9-volt battery snap,
   2 alligator clips,
   several inches of
   electrical wire

☐ Patience!

WHAT TO DO:

STEP 1 ▶ This experiment can be as simple as choosing a salsa, pouring about a half cup into a jar or bowl, placing a steel rod inside, and letting it sit for a long, LONG time. Check the rod periodically to see if there's any evidence of corrosion, which would look like little indentations in the rod. You can try different salsa brands on different rods to see if one is better than another — just be sure to put the rods in the right salsa when you're finished observing them. Refresh the salsa in the jar whenever it gets to the point of smelling really bad or looking especially moldy.

STEP 2 ▶ If you want to try what Jamie did, you can use electricity to speed up your reaction (though it will still take a long time!). This is where the battery, the battery snap, and the alligator clips come in. You can create a circuit from the battery that will flow through the steel, into the salsa, and back to the battery. This may help pull material away from the bar.

To set up a DC current through your bar, connect the battery snap to the battery. Then connect the wire end of 2 alligator clips to your 6-volt battery by clipping one end of your alligator clips to the terminals. Connect the negative terminal to the steel bar. If your clip isn't big enough to grasp the bar, you can use some stripped electrical wire connected to the clip to wrap around the bar. Metal must be touching metal from the clip to the wire to the bar.

Set your steel bar into a half cup of salsa and be sure it can sit without tipping over. Place the other alligator clip into the salsa. It doesn't have to be pushed in far as long as the metal is in contact with the salsa. You might see small bubbles form in the salsa; this just means the current is successfully flowing through the circuit. Be careful not to touch the bar while your circuit is running. The current isn't strong enough to be dangerous, but it's enough to give you a good shock.

STEP 3 To check on the progress of your salsa, first remove the clip from the salsa and then remove the bar. After making your observations, reset your bar as you did in the last step.

STEP 4 Let your experiment run as long as you can until you see definitive results or are convinced nothing is happening. You will probably want to replace the salsa in the jars weekly, which means you'll need several jars of each salsa you test.

What Happened?

Salt and acid are corrosive to metals, and these are 2 of the ingredients in salsa. They won't wear away the metal quickly, but they can wear it away. The current from a DC source will cause the metal to lose electrons into the salsa, which is another REALLY slow way to reduce the amount of metal in the bar. But, if you've got nothing but time on your hands, you might just be able to combine the effects of these 2 factors and get this technique to work.

WHAT'S YOUR CONCLUSION?

☐ **Confirmed**
☐ **Plausible**
☐ **Busted**

IS TOILET PAPER REALLY STRONG ENOUGH TO HELP A PRISONER ESCAPE FROM JAIL?

If you can get through your prison bars with salsa, what happens if your cell is on the top floor? How can a jailbird get down to the ground if he doesn't know how to fly? You'd need something to act like a rope you can climb down. One thing you'd have access to that's long enough is toilet paper. But is TP actually strong enough to get this dirty job done?

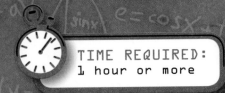

TIME REQUIRED:
1 hour or more

WHAT YOU'LL NEED: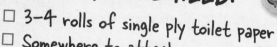

- ☐ 3-4 rolls of single ply toilet paper
- ☐ Somewhere to attach your rope, like a chin-up bar, jungle gym, or tree branch
- ☐ An adult to spot you

WHAT TO DO:

STEP 1 ▶ Fashioning your toilet paper into a rope may sound simple, but it will require a lot of patience. The idea is to create a series of TP strings that you can braid together into a stronger rope. It's possible to tie the ends of your ropes together if your TP breaks while you work, but it'll work better if you can keep your strands in one piece.

Start by attaching 1 end of a roll of toilet paper to something solid. You could use a doorknob, table or chair leg, or some other piece of furniture, or you could have a partner hold the end for you. Once the end is secured, begin twisting the toilet paper tightly (but gently!) to create your first strand. Decide how long you want the rope to be. Fifteen to twenty feet should be more than enough. When you reach the end, be sure to hold it in place with something heavy so the strand doesn't unwind. Make at least 3 strands of the same length in this way; 4 would be better.

STEP 2 ▶ Create a rope by weaving your individual strands together. Tie the strands together at one end and as tightly (and gently!) as possible, braid your strands from that end to the other. When you reach the end, tie the strings together again to keep your rope intact. You may need to try this several times before you get your technique down.

STEP 3 ▶ Once you've successfully braided your rope into a single, tight strand, find a place to see if it will hold your weight. We recommend you have an adult with you to spot you as you do this, so you don't hit the ground too hard if your rope breaks. Find a way to attach your rope to something about 6 to 10 feet off the ground. You can tie one end to the structure, but it'll be easier to loop it around the object you're using and to hold both ends in your hands. Make sure your spotter is nearby, and then see if you can hold the rope and lift your feet off the ground.

Was toilet paper up to this job, or would you be trapped in your cell indefinitely?

WHAT'S YOUR CONCLUSION?

☐ **Confirmed**

☐ **Plausible**

☐ **Busted**

ARE BED SHEETS STRONG ENOUGH TO HELP A PRISONER ESCAPE FROM JAIL?

Is the prison warden keeping close track of how much toilet paper you're using? If so, you've got one more shot at getting down to the ground from your cell: bed sheets! If you can tie them together and get a good grip, this plan could bring the freedom you've been dreaming of.

WHAT YOU'LL NEED:

- ☐ 2 bed sheets
- ☐ Somewhere to attach your rope like a chin-up bar, jungle gym, or tree branch
- ☐ An adult to spot you

TIME REQUIRED:
15 minutes

WHAT TO DO:

STEP 1 It's not too hard to make a rope out of your bed sheets. Since you'd probably only have two in your cell, that's how many you should work with. You can try 2 different options: one is to tie the ends of the sheets together for a *longer* rope; the other is to wrap and tie the sheets together to make a *stronger* rope.

Whichever technique you try — and why not try both? — we recommend tying knots into the sheet at one foot intervals. This will shorten your rope but make it much easier for you to get a good grip.

STEP 2 Attach your rope to something. You can tie it from one end or loop it over the object and hold both ends. Have someone spot you and see if you can hold onto the rope and lift your feet off the ground. If you succeed, see if you can climb the rope using the knots you tied in it. Just be sure not to climb your rope without an adult spotting you in case you slip.

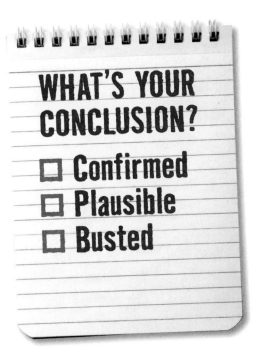

WHAT'S YOUR CONCLUSION?

☐ **Confirmed**
☐ **Plausible**
☐ **Busted**

What Happened?

The strength of all materials is combined when they're wrapped into a fiber of some sort. Think of yarn or twine — the strand you hold in your hand is always made of sets of smaller strands wound together, and the final material is much stronger than the individual fibers. This is true for toilet paper, too. If you're careful enough when you braid your TP together, you can create a cord that's strong enough to hold your weight, and there's enough fabric wound together in a full bed sheet that it can hold the weight of a person.

TRY THIS:

USE THE POWER OF ANTACIDS TO LAUNCH A ROCKET.

Usually antacids are taken to save us from stomach pain, but supposedly they once saved a person from the confines of his jail cell. According to this myth, a prisoner saved up antacid tablets for years and then wet them all at once. The gas produced was so great it burst through his cell walls and allowed him to escape. Adam and Jamie determined that if it were possible to collect enough antacid tablets to break open the cell, the person inside would never be able to survive, so the myth was BUSTED. But the gaseous strength of antacids is indisputably strong. Here's another way to harness the propulsion power that can follow the plop of a little pill into water.

WHAT YOU'LL NEED:

- [ ] 1 package of fizzing antacid tablets
- [ ] Water
- [ ] 1 empty film canister with a top that fits inside the canister, not around the top
- [ ] 1 8 1/2 x 11 sheet of paper
- [ ] 1 roll of cellophane tape
- [ ] 1 pair of scissors
- [ ] Eye protection
- [ ] A big, open space for your launch pad

TIME REQUIRED: 20 minutes

WHAT TO DO:

STEP 1 ▶ The film canister will be your fuel cell. Use the paper to construct the body of your rocket around this cell. Cut the paper in half the long way, and wrap one piece around the film canister so it's covered and the opening of the canister faces out. Use the tape to secure the paper.

STEP 2 ▶ From the other half of the paper, cut a circle that's as large as possible. You can trace the bottom of a bottle or jar to create a good circle. Cut away a quarter of the circle (a section that would cover from 12 o'clock to 3 o'clock on a clock face) and fold the remaining 3/4 circle to form a cone by connecting the edges where the section was removed. Use the tape to secure the cone. This will be the nose of your rocket.

STEP 3 ▶ Now cut four triangles. Each should have a long side that's about 3 1/2 inches long and a short side that's about 2 inches long. You can cut out 2 3 1/2 x 2-inch rectangles, and then cut along the diagonal to make your 4 triangles. These triangles can be used to make fins for your rocket.

STEP 4 ▶ Use the tape to attach the nose to the free end of your rocket body, and attach the fins to the end with the canister so the short leg is even with the canister's mouth and the long leg is connected to the rocket body. The diagonal side faces away from the rocket.

STEP 5 ▶ Find a big, open space to launch your rocket. You should be somewhere outdoors for adequate space and to prevent making a mess inside. Put on your eye protection. Hold your rocket upside down and remove the lid from the film canister. Fill the canister 1/3 of the way full with water and drop one antacid tablet into the canister. Quickly replace the lid and set the rocket down so it's ready to launch.

BLAST OFF!

You can experiment with creating the lightest rocket possible, changing the rocket design, and using slightly more antacid. Remember, the less your rocket weighs, the higher it will fly, and adding too much antacid will just make it harder to cap the fuel cell and position your rocket before the cell blasts, so don't put in too many tablets at once.

WHAT'S YOUR CONCLUSION?

☐ **Confirmed**
☐ **Plausible**
☐ **Busted**

What Happened?

Antacids are designed to neutralize stomach acid and reduce digestive discomfort. One ingredient that helps this process is sodium bicarbonate (baking soda), which forms carbon dioxide gas when it combines with water. If this gas is contained, pressure will build as the volume of gas increases. You'd need a lot of carbon dioxide gas to bust out of a jail cell, but just one tablet will shoot a model rocket into the air.

93

IS FALLING FROM A GREAT HEIGHT INTO WATER JUST AS DANGEROUS AS FALLING ONTO CEMENT?

If you fell from the top of a house — or, better yet, an airplane — into water, could it do as much damage as hitting solid pavement? That's the claim in this myth. Since water, like a solid, doesn't compress under pressure, it stands to reason that an object or person falling on water would hit just as hard as hitting the pavement. Does that smack of the truth to you?

WHAT YOU'LL NEED:

- ☐ Items for dropping, 2 of each. We recommend:
    - ☐ Clay
    - ☐ Eggs
    - ☐ Ripe tomatoes
    - ☐ Apples
    - ☐ Water balloons
- ☐ I body of water. Could be a bathtub, pool, aquarium, pot, or bucket.
- ☐ I paved surface
- ☐ I camera (optional)

TIME REQUIRED: 20 minutes

WHAT TO DO:

STEP 1 ▶ Choose your objects and the location you'll drop them from. You can simply drop them from your hands into your bucket or bathtub, or you can use a ladder or window to increase the height of your drop. If you're up more than a few feet high, make sure that you'll be able to aim into your water source and that the water will be deep enough that the objects won't touch bottom.

We recommend using clay balls for at least one of your objects. The clay ball will change shape with impact and hold that shape, which will make comparing the results much easier. For low drops, you can use a ball the size of a tennis ball. For more extreme heights, you can increase the size of the ball. The other good thing about using clay is that you can reshape the balls and retry your drop.

STEP 2 ▶ Now drop the object from the same height onto pavement. Simply let the object drop from your hand; you don't want to add force by throwing it down. Observe the change in the object. You could draw what you see, or take photos to record your results for comparison later.

STEP 3 ▶ Drop the same type of object, from the same height, into water. Observe the change in the object and compare it to the change in the object dropped onto pavement. Were both objects damaged? Was the impact of the pavement far greater than that of water?

WHAT'S YOUR CONCLUSION?

☐ **Confirmed**
☐ **Plausible**
☐ **Busted**

TRY THIS: MAKE YOUR OWN CATAPULT.

Catapults have turned up in a couple of *MythBusters* myths. Whether the catapult was formed from a tree or a boom lift, they were big enough to give a full-grown man the ride of his life. We won't tell you how to build something that can fling people, but small catapults put physics to work and are still lots of fun. Here are 2 procedures, 1 easy and 1 more advanced, for making a catapult of your own.

Catapult Method 1: EASY

WHAT YOU'LL NEED: $

- ☐ 1 large empty tape dispenser
- ☐ Strong tape or glue
- ☐ 1 sheet of 8 1/2 × 11-inch paper
- ☐ Rubber bands
- ☐ 1 spoon
- ☐ 1 piece of wood or a cutting board

TIME REQUIRED:
15 minutes

WHAT TO DO:

STEP 1 ▶ Using tape or glue, attach the tape dispenser to the middle of your piece of wood or cutting board. Make sure the dispenser is firmly held in place. If you're using tape, run the tape through the spaces in the dispenser and around the bottom of the board.

STEP 2 ▶ Make a short, tight roll of paper by folding the sheet in half the long way and then in half the long way a second time. When you're done, you'll have a 8 1/2 x 2 1/2 inch rectangle. Roll this rectangle up the long way, insert it into the center of your tape dispenser, and let it go. The paper will unwind and fill up the space. You'll attach your rubber bands by wrapping them around the ends of the paper roll.

STEP 3 ▶ Attach the spoon with the top of the spoon facing away from the tape dispenser to the curved side of the dispenser. Place a rubber band around one side of the paper, across the spoon, and then loop it around the other side of the paper. Use several rubber bands so the spoon is held snugly. If the rubber bands are too long, you can twist them after looping the second time and pull them back around to first side of the paper.

STEP 4 ▶ Once your spoon is in place, your catapult is ready. Find small objects like coins, cotton balls, or marshmallows and see how far you can get them to fly.

Catapult Method 2: ADVANCED

WHAT YOU'LL NEED:

- ☐ 1 medium-sized (approximately 1 foot square) heavy piece of wood
- ☐ 2 small pieces of wood, approximately 1 x 4 inches and 1 inch thick
- ☐ 1 hammer
- ☐ 2 nails
- ☐ 1 saw
- ☐ 2 dowels — one 2 or 3 inches wider than your base and ½ inch thick or less, the other 6–8 inches long and about half as thick as the first.
- ☐ 1 drill
- ☐ 2 small scraps of wood
- ☐ Wood glue
- ☐ 1 hot glue gun
- ☐ 1 plastic or paper cup, 4 oz
- ☐ 2 hook screws
- ☐ 1 rubber band
- ☐ An adult to help you

TIME REQUIRED:
45 minutes

WHAT TO DO:

STEP 1 The largest piece of wood will act as the base of your catapult. Make sure it's heavy enough to stay in place when you depress the catapult. If necessary, you can weigh it down with stones, bricks, or books, or hold it in place with one hand.

Ask your adult to help you use the drill to make holes at the top of the posts that face each other. The holes should be wide enough for the long dowel to fit in them and rotate smoothly.

STEP 2 Use the hammer and nails to attach the 2 smaller pieces of wood to opposite sides of the outside of your base so they stand up like goal posts.

STEP 3 Place the dowel so it passes through both posts, extending across the base. Use your saw to cut the ends so they only stick out past the posts about a half inch. Use the wood glue or hammer and nails to attach the small pieces of wood to the ends of the dowel to prevent it from slipping out of the posts.

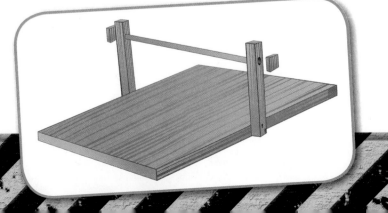

STEP 4 In the center of the dowel, drill a small hole that's wide enough for the second dowel to fit through. Place the second dowel through this hole and position it so one end rests against the base at about a 45-degree angle and the other end sticks out about 5 inches past the longer dowel. Use the glue to secure the position of the dowels against each other (make sure the end touching the base is free to move).

STEP 5 Use the glue to attach the cup to the top of the second dowel so that it opens up at an angle. You might decide to cut the cup if the sides are more than 1–2 inches high.

STEP 6 Use the glue or drill a hole in the second dowel to attach a hook screw so the curve of the hook opens toward the cup. Screw the other hook into the edge of the base on the side of the long dowel, so that the short dowel rests with the curve of the hook opening away from the catapult.

STEP 7 Hook the ends of the rubber band around the 2 hooks. It should stretch and fit snugly. If not, find a shorter rubber band.

Your catapult is ready! Pull the end of the short dowel with the cup down toward the base to cock the catapult and place and object (like a marshmallow or cotton balls) in the cup. When the tension feels strong, release the dowel and watch your object fly!

 CAN ARMOR MADE OUT OF PAPER REALLY PROTECT YOU?

When metal technologies advance, the first place they're put to use is in armor. But were things ever so simple that paper was the best choice available? It sounds suspicious, but ancient Chinese warriors really did use paper for their armor. It wasn't the only type of armor they wore — steel armor was available, too — but according to this myth, the paper armor was stronger than the steel. Here are some simple tests you can do to determine how paper's strength compares to steel's.

WHAT YOU'LL NEED:

- ☐ Mulberry paper*
- ☐ 12-inch square steel plate, 1/4 inch thick or less**
- ☐ Clay block (approximately 6 inches on a side)
- ☐ 1 hammer
- ☐ 1 nail

*Mulberry paper can be purchased online or at art supply stores. It usually comes in 57 x 30 inch sheets.

**Steel plates can be purchased online.

TIME REQUIRED:
30 minutes

WHAT TO DO:

Kari, Grant, and Tory did the hard work on this one. A historian told them that the Chinese definitely used paper armor around 2,600 years ago. They also learned the techniques that people believe were used to make the paper into armor, and that mulberry paper was the paper of choice. The thick, cloth-like quality of mulberry paper gave it special strength. Some historians said the paper was shellacked; some said it was sewn into cotton covers; and some said it was simply folded over itself into a square. After testing all of the techniques to see which was the strongest (using equipment we're pretty sure you don't have at home), the MythBusters determined that the folded paper was the strongest. This makes your experiment a lot easier!

STEP 1 ▸ You need to create a folded piece of mulberry paper that represents one piece of armor. The folded paper should be half an inch thick when you're finished, and you should be able to get this thickness using one sheet of mulberry paper. Fold the paper in half 4 or 5 times. Then turn the paper and repeat this until you have a small block. You can use a rubber band to keep the block from unfolding. This stack is what you'll be testing for strength.

STEP 2 ▸ You're going to test your steel and paper against at least 2 types of assault: a blunt weapon, like a club or mace, and a sharp object, like an arrow or spear. Your hammer will serve as the blunt object, and the hammer and nail will act as the sharp object.

You'll use the clay to indicate how much protection the steel or paper provided against attack. Comparing the marks left on the clay will give you a good idea of what might have happened to a body that was being protected with the techniques you're testing.

Place the steel plate over one clay block and the paper plate over the other. First, try hitting each with the hammer. Pretend you're a soldier and the clay is your enemy, but make sure you're careful not to hit anything (or anyone!) besides your tests. Bring the hammer down on one and then the other of your armors, and then move them aside to see the damage. You can also hit one of the clay blocks without protection to see what would happen to someone who wasn't wearing armor.

STEP 3 You can use the same clay blocks without reshaping them, or you can take some time to reshape the blocks before testing the next scenario. Once your blocks are ready, replace the steel and paper plates and get your nail. Hold the nail onto the armor and give it as strong a hit with the hammer as you can, being careful to avoid hitting your fingers. Hitting the clay like this won't do as much damage as an arrow shot from a bow would, but it'll give you an idea of the protection provided by the armor. Once you've hit both plates with the hammer and nail, remove them and check out the clay. What happened this time?

You've run the tests, so what do you think? Could paper armor possibly have been the protection of choice in 600 BCE?

What Happened?

Between the fibers of the paper and the layering of the armor, paper is actually strong enough to stop most blows — at least the ones a soldier was likely to meet in 600 BCE. Plus, if you're looking for something that's easy to move around in, paper wins easily when compared to metal. The biggest downside with paper is its inability to withstand water, so just be sure to schedule your battles for sunny days!

WHAT'S YOUR CONCLUSION?

☐ **Confirmed**

☐ **Plausible**

☐ **Busted**

TRY THIS: MAKE YOUR OWN PAPER ARMOR.

Want to make paper armor and see what it feels like to wear? Here's a plan to put together proper paper protection.

WHAT YOU'LL NEED:

- ☐ Lots of paper*
- ☐ Cotton cord or yarn
- ☐ Lots of rubber bands
- ☐ I power drill
- ☐ I adult to help with the drill

TIME REQUIRED:
5-10 hours or more

*You can use the mulberry paper to build your armor, but it will be expensive and harder to work with. Since you're not actually going into battle, we recommend you use standard 8 ½ x 11 inch printer paper or construction paper.

WARNING:

Make sure to get an adult's help with this experiment. You should never use power tools on your own.

14.4V

WHAT TO DO:

STEP 1 ▶ You need to make the scales for your armor first. Take a piece of paper and fold it in half the long way twice, and then fold it in half the other way once. This should give you a rectangle of paper that's approximately 3 x 4 inches. Place a rubber band around the paper to hold it in place and repeat this until you have all the squares you need.

How many squares do you need? It depends on how big you are. Kari's suit of armor was made from about 170 squares: 58 front and back, and 25 for each sleeve. The front and back were 10 rows long and the sleeves were 4 rows. If you're 5 feet tall or shorter, we recommend using 7 or 8 rows for the front and back, and 2 or 3 rows for the sleeves. This means you'll need about 130 squares.

STEP 2 ▶ All the squares will need holes in each of the four corners. This will allow you to tie them, top and bottom, to other scales. Use the drill (and an adult's help!) to put holes in the corners of the squares.

STEP 3 ▶ Make the four main pieces of armor (front, back, and two sleeves) by tying together squares of paper in rows. The front and back should have 1 row of 5 to protect your chest, 5 rows of 7 to protect your body, and 2 rows of 3 to protect your groin. Start with the top row and use the cotton cord or yarn to tie the paper together. The middle square of each row should be on top of the others, and the squares to the right and left should each be layered the square closer to the center.

Once you have all your rows completed, connect them moving from top to bottom. Each row should be connected under the row above them.

STEP 4 Once you have all 4 plates ready, it's time to tie them together. Connect the front and back with the yarn or cotton cord by tying the top and outermost holes of the front to the back. Leave plenty of room between the ties to pull the armor over your head. If you want to make the armor more comfortable, you could use fabric strips instead of yarn to connect the front and back.

Connect the sleeves by attaching the top and outermost corner holes to the SECOND hole on the front and back of the main plates. This prevents any vulnerable area at the top of your torso from being exposed. The bottom outermost holes can be attached to the holes on the main plates that are closest to them. Make the ties as tight as you can while making sure you can fit into the armor.

You can decide if you want to decorate the armor or go out with a simple suit. And that's it — you're ready for battle.

MYTH

WILL A BOAT MADE OUT OF WOOD SHAVINGS AND WATER REALLY FLOAT?

Rumor has it that during World War II, an aircraft carrier was constructed out of a new material called pykrete. Pykrete is a mixture of wood shavings and water, called an ice alloy, and it was reputed to be bulletproof, stronger than ice, and slow to melt. And it would clearly cost a lot less than the price of the usual boatbuilding materials. But could anything built out of an ice alloy really be seaworthy?

WHAT YOU'LL NEED:

$ $

- ☐ Water
- ☐ 5-6 lbs. of wood shavings*
- ☐ 1 freezer
- ☐ 1 paper plate
- ☐ 1 scale
- ☐ 1 large bucket or trash can
- ☐ 1 measuring cup
- ☐ 6 large, shallow disposable aluminum baking pans (or 2 for each trial you plan to prepare simultaneously)
- ☐ 1 bathtub or kiddie pool
- ☐ 1 notebook (for recording your results)

*Wood shavings can be purchased from pet supply stores as bedding material.

TIME REQUIRED:
30 minutes for mixing;
overnight for freezing;
20 minutes for testing;
2-3 hours melting

WHAT TO DO:

STEP 1 Pykrete is a mixture of wood shavings and water with 14% wood shavings. To make your pykrete mixture, for each gallon of water you use, add approximately 1 7/10 pounds of wood shavings. Use your scale and a paper plate to weigh your shavings, and then combine them and the water in a large bucket or trashcan. Mix the pykrete thoroughly with your hands, making sure all the wood shavings are wet and that there are no clumps.

How much mixture you make will depend on how many trials you want to run. We have 3 suggestions for you, which means you'd need enough pykrete to fill 3 of your baking pans. You can try these tests one after the other if you prepare several trays at once, or you can use 2 pans and simply remake the trays each time you use them.

STEP 2 Pour your pykrete into 1 baking pan and water into another. Place the pans in the freezer and keep them there overnight, or for at least 12 hours.

STEP 3 Remove a pan of ice and one of pykrete from the freezer, and take the ice and pykrete out of the aluminum. Only remove the pans you will be using immediately.

STEP 4 The first test is to see which substance melts faster. Bring your ice and pykrete pans to a room at regular temperature. Remove the ice and pykrete from their pans and prop the frozen blocks at one end, to create an L shape. Leave the blocks to melt — the pans will collect the water. You may need to place something at the bottom of the frozen blocks, like a can of soup, to keep them from falling down. About every 30 minutes, pour whatever water has collected into a measuring cup. Keep track of how much water each pan is losing. After several hours, record which has lost more water: the ice or the pykrete.

STEP 5 The next step is to discover whether the pykrete will float. Fill a kiddie pool or bathtub halfway with lukewarm water. Take another pan of ice and one of pykrete from the freezer and remove the frozen blocks from their trays. Set both afloat in the pool of water. Every 15 minutes, observe the 2 blocks and compare them. Is one melting faster than the other? If you had to set sail on one, which would it be?

STEP 6 Take another pan of ice and pykrete out of the freezer. This time, you'll test how solid each substance is. Take the pans outside to a paved area, like a driveway or sidewalk. Make sure you're wearing long pants in case the blocks shatter and hit your legs. Hold 1 block above your head and let it drop to the ground. Repeat this procedure with the other block. Did one substance hold together better than the other?

So, what do you think? Would you want to set sail in a pykrete vessel?

WHAT'S YOUR CONCLUSION?

☐ **Confirmed**
☐ **Plausible**
☐ **Busted**

What Happened?

Ice has a specific arrangement of molecules that's easy to disrupt under force. This breaks the bonds between the molecules and cracks the ice apart. When a new substance, like wood shavings, is added to the water and frozen, that material can actually absorb some of the force and bend rather than simply snapping apart. The material in the ice also insulates it from the warmer surrounding temperatures, which keeps it frozen longer, and even allows cracks to fill and refreeze with water from the outside. All in all, you wind up with something stronger and longer lasting than frozen water on its own.

TRY THIS: MAKE YOUR OWN TORNADO.

WHAT YOU'LL NEED:

$ $

- ☐ 1 square foot of wood
- ☐ 1 pencil
- ☐ 1 disposable plastic bowl or serving dish with flat bottom and sides, about 4–6 inches across. Take-out soup containers work well.
- ☐ 1 glue gun
- ☐ 2 identical clear, thin vinyl sheets (thin enough to roll but thick enough to stay vertical), slightly under 1 square foot each*
- ☐ Water
- ☐ 1 measuring cup
- ☐ 1 clear plastic saucer from a plant pot, at least 8 inches across
- ☐ 1 small handheld fan
- ☐ Dry ice**
- ☐ 1 pair of thick gloves
- ☐ 1 hammer
- ☐ An adult

Whether they're chasing the storms or building something to protect themselves from them, Jamie and Adam have had some interesting experiences with tornados. But what about seeing how they actually form? Get ready to make a tornado right in the comfort of your own home!

*You should be able to find vinyl sheets at your local hardware store.

**Some supermarkets carry dry ice. Do an Internet search to find the closest place to you. You'll need to keep the blocks in a Styrofoam container. Blocks cost about a dollar a pound in increments of 10 pounds and will last about a day before melting completely.

WARNING:

Dry ice is solid carbon dioxide. It isn't toxic, but it is VERY cold. Always handle dry ice with thick gloves, like gardening gloves. Do NOT use rubber or latex gloves — they won't protect you adequately from the cold. Never touch dry ice with bare skin and never eat dry ice — you risk getting very badly burned. Dry ice is completely safe if it is handled correctly.

WARNING:

Make sure to get an adult's help with this experiment. You should never use a glue gun on your own.

TIME REQUIRED:
1 hour

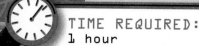

WHAT TO DO:

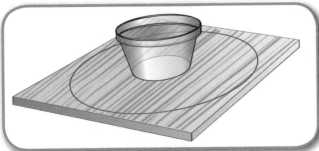

STEP 1 Build your tornado chamber. The wood will be the base of your chamber. First, use a pencil to lightly trace the outline of the plant saucer on the base. Then, ask your adult to help you use the glue gun to attach the serving dish or bowl in the center of the wood. Next, glue the edge of one piece of vinyl to one side of the dish. When the glue is set, curve the vinyl around the bowl without touching the bowl again, so the other edge is just inside the pencil tracing you drew earlier. Now glue it in place on the base. Glue the edge of the second piece of vinyl to the dish opposite where the first piece is glued. Bend the second piece in the same direction around the bowl as the first, making an identical shape, and then glue it in place. Your vinyl pieces should now look like a partial spiral from the center bowl. Check to make sure the plant saucer can be placed upside-down over the vinyl to form a cover.

STEP 2 Cut a hole in the center of the plant saucer that's about 3 inches across. Your tornado chamber is ready!

STEP 3 Find a safe place — like a garage or an outdoor space — and use the hammer to break off some small pieces of the dry ice. Remember to keep your gloves on when handling the dry ice.

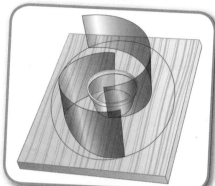

STEP 4 Put a half cup of water in the dish in the center of the tornado chamber. Add a few pieces of dry ice and place the plant saucer top over the vinyl. Turn on the fan and hold it at the hole in the top so it is blowing away from the chamber. The more the back of the fan can connect with the chamber, the better air current you'll be able to generate. You should have a tornado whipped up in no time!

What Happened?

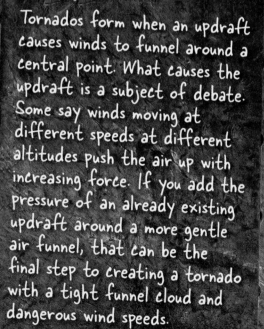

Tornados form when an updraft causes winds to funnel around a central point. What causes the updraft is a subject of debate. Some say winds moving at different speeds at different altitudes push the air up with increasing force. If you add the pressure of an already existing updraft around a more gentle air funnel, that can be the final step to creating a tornado with a tight funnel cloud and dangerous wind speeds.

TRY THIS: MAKE YOUR OWN LIGHTNING.

Not satisfied with just the funnel cloud? Everyone knows lightning is another important part of any impressive storm. Here's how you can act like Thor and create your own impressive thunderbolts.

Adam with the MythBusters' hurricane machine.

TIME REQUIRED: 10 minutes

WHAT YOU'LL NEED: 💲

☐ 1 steel or iron pot (not aluminum)
☐ 1 pair of rubber gloves
☐ 1 plastic sheet (like a plastic bag or table cloth)
☐ 1 roll of cellophane tape
☐ 1 steel or iron fork (not aluminum)

WHAT TO DO:

STEP 1 ▷ Tape the plastic sheet to a tabletop so it stays in place.

STEP 2 Place the pot on the plastic sheet and put on the rubber gloves. Holding the pot by the handles, rub it back and forth quickly on the plastic for about a minute.

STEP 3 Darken the room so you can see the lightning better. Bring the fork slowly to the edge of the pot. When it gets close enough, you should see a spark jump from the pot to the fork. Did you hear a crackle, too? That's the sound that would be thunder if your experiment were life-sized!

What Happened?

Lightning is the movement of a static electrical charge from one place to another. It's the same kind of thing you experience when you touch someone while wearing socks on a carpet and get a shock. In nature, the static charges build up in clouds, and when they get close enough to the ground or another cloud, the charge jumps from one place to another, making the bright light we see as lightning. The vibrations of the air caused by the movement and heat of the lightning are what we hear as thunder.

TRY THIS: MAKE YOUR OWN TSUNAMI.

Remember the myth about using an explosion to create a wave you can surf on? That myth was busted because the water was too deep, and the explosion would have needed to be REALLY big. The explosion was cool, but the surfing was a bust. However, one thing that does make big waves is a tsunami. Making a model of a tsunami helps us understand how they work, and it also makes us think about how to prepare for them. Follow the steps in this experiment and see if you get a wave that's big enough to hang 10.

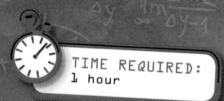

TIME REQUIRED:
1 hour

WARNING:

Make sure to get an adult's help if you use a drill with this experiment. You should never use power tools on your own.

WHAT YOU'LL NEED:

☐ 1 large aquarium or tub, at least 3 feet long, the narrower the better
☐ 1 or more desk, door, or table hinges and screw to fit
☐ 1 drill or screwdriver
☐ 2 pieces of wood that can lie width-wise in the tank, about 3 inches wide and ½–1 inch thick
☐ 1 thin board, about 1 foot long or longer (no more than ⅓ the length of your tank)
☐ 1 tube of aquarium glue
☐ Water
☐ Hammer and nail with a broad top
☐ String or wire
☐ Water

WHAT TO DO:

Tsunamis form when there's an earthquake under the ocean. The movement of the ocean floor creates a wave that moves toward shore. As the wave moves into shallow water, it picks up height and speed, which is what causes damage on land when it hits. Your model will include a hinged piece of wood on one side that will simulate the movement of the Earth during an earthquake, and a sloping piece of wood on the other that will simulate the shore. You'll want the water to be fairly shallow — about 6 inches deep will be plenty — because the deeper the water, the weaker the waves.

STEP 1 Attach the two boards together with the hinges by screwing them onto both boards. The boards will lay at one end of the tank with the hinges positioned so you can lift one of the boards from one side while the other board holds it in place along the bottom. Make sure your hinges are positioned correctly before you attach the screws.

Use a hammer to put a nail most of the way into the top board, and then tie the string or wire to the nail. You'll use the string to pull up on the board and create your earthquake. The string or wire should be long enough to reach well out of the water, at least a foot or two.

STEP 2 Use a brick, rock, or sand to prop the thin board up along the opposite edge of the tank so that it rests a few inches above the water line. The other end of the board should slope down toward the middle of the tank so its base forms a 30-degree angle with the bottom of the tank. Use the aquarium glue to fix the board to the bottom and side of the tank in this position. The sides of the board do not have to reach the sides of the tank, and it's fine if water gets below it.

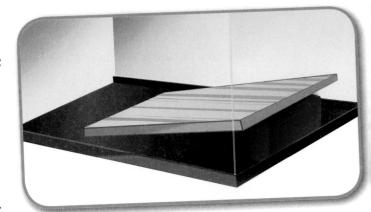

STEP 3 Once the glue has had a chance to dry, fill the tank with about 6 inches of water. Be sure to leave the end of the shore above the water line. Then pull up on the string to raise the board and cause waves. Try different ways of pulling the board up: faster and slower; higher and lower. What effect does it have on the waves formed on your shore line?

You can go further with this by placing objects along your shoreline and observing what effect the waves you generate have on them. Try placing small rocks or models of buildings on the other end of the tank. What if you use clay to create an interesting shoreline? How much can you learn from your model about the impact of tsunami waves once they reach land?

TRY THIS: MAKE YOUR OWN SEISMOMETER.

The MythBusters examined a story about a mythical earthquake machine. Nikola Tesla, a scientist who lived from 1856 until 1943, was said to have built a tool that could cause an earthquake-like effect in buildings and other objects. The team determined a tool like this probably never existed, but we can tell you how to build a tool that can detect an earthquake if a real one comes.

WHAT YOU'LL NEED:

☐ I cardboard box, about a foot tall
☐ I plastic cup
☐ String
☐ I pair of scissors
☐ Coins, nuts and bolts, small rocks, sand, or marbles
☐ I marker
☐ Clay
☐ Paper

TIME REQUIRED:
20 minutes

WHAT TO DO:

A seismometer is a tool that can detect movements and make a visible record of them. Scientific seismometers are so sensitive that they can detect incredibly small movements in the Earth. Your seismometer won't be that sensitive, but you might be able to use it to see if you really do shake the house when you run around.

STEP 1 Cut the top off a cardboard box, so that your box has a bottom and 4 sides but nothing to close at the top. Then turn the box on its side, so the open side faces forward with cardboard above and below it, like a cave.

STEP 2 Use your scissors to make 2 small holes in what is now the top of the box. The holes should be in the center and about 2 inches apart.

STEP 3 Take your plastic cup and poke a single hole in the center of its bottom. Make 2 holes opposite each other at the top of the cup.

STEP 4 ▶ Place the marker through the hole in the bottom of the cup so that it sticks out a few inches. Use the clay to hold the marker in place by pressing it around the marker on the inside of the cup. Then fill the cup about 2/3 full with the coins, marbles, stones, or nuts and bolts.

STEP 5 ▶ Thread the string through the holes at the top of the cup so the cup will hang from them. Then thread the other ends of the string through the holes in the box so the cup hangs inside the box. Tie the strings so the marker just touches the base of the box when the cap is off.

STEP 6 ▶ Place your seismometer on the floor and take the cap off the marker. Place a sheet of paper under the marker so the paper edge climbs up the back of the box. While someone runs or jumps around the room, slowly pull the paper under the marker toward you and out of the box. The movements of the box will cause the pen to bounce and make squiggles. The bigger the squiggle, the stronger the movement.

What do you think would shake the box more: you and your friends, or an actual earthquake?

MYTH

CAN HELIUM BALLOONS REALLY LIFT A CHILD INTO THE SKY?

How many times have you seen a movie where a child floats off into the sky, holding a bunch of helium balloons? Are these party toys really a threat to earthbound kids, or would the number of balloons needed to lift a child be more than he or she could handle?

WHAT YOU'LL NEED:

☐ Standard, 11-inch balloons filled with helium, at least 10, with ribbon or string ties

☐ 1 box of paper clips

☐ 1 scale

TIME REQUIRED:
45 minutes

WHAT TO DO:

STEP 1

The trick to this experiment is to determine how much weight balloons can lift and to use that number to calculate how many balloons would be needed to lift different items, like a child.

Tie your 10 balloons together by their ribbons. If you have extra balloons, keep them on hand in case one of your test balloons breaks. Take 1 ribbon and tie a loop at the bottom of it. Take your paper clips and hook one onto the ribbon loop. Start making a chain of paper clips connected to the balloon string — the chain can be branched or have several parallel lengths. Each time you add a paper clip, carefully let go of the balloons to see if they will lift.

Continue adding paperclips until the balloons will no longer lift into the air when you let them go. Count how many paper clips the balloon was able to lift with.

STEP 2

You need to know how much 1 paper clip weighs. It should be about 1 gram, but if you have a scale, you should check it. If you have a sensitive kitchen scale, you can try taking the mass of 1 paper clip. If that's too light to register on the scale, add the paper clips to the scale in multiples of 10 until it's heavy enough to register. To find the mass of a single paper clip, divide the mass of all the paper clips by the number you placed there.

If your scale gave you a measurement in pounds, mark it down. If it gave you the mass in grams, divide this number by 453.6 to find the mass in pounds. This is how much your 10 balloons can lift. Divide 10 by that number to find out how many balloons would be needed to lift 1 pound.

STEP 3 So, how many balloons would it take to lift a 50-pound child? Multiply the number of balloons needed to lift 1 pound by 50, and you've got the answer. Do you think a carnival even has that many balloons?

If you want to make a fun display about this, find the mass of a bunch of different objects and calculate how many balloons would be needed to lift each one. Place the objects or images of the objects on a table with labels explaining how many balloons would lift them. Does your favorite toy weigh 5 pounds? Does your cat weigh 10 pounds? What about your best friend? How many balloons would each one need to get the ride of their life?

WHAT'S YOUR CONCLUSION?
☐ **Confirmed**
☐ **Plausible**
☐ **Busted**

TRY THIS: MAKE YOUR OWN METAL DETECTOR.

Saying something is like finding a needle in a haystack probably means it's really hard to do. If you saw the *MythBusters* team working on this myth, then you know they confirmed it. Even with some handy needle-finding devices, Jamie and Adam needed more than 6 hours to find four needles in a haystack.

We're pretty sure you don't need us to tell you how to try doing this on your own. But we thought we might make it a little easier on you. What if you were searching for that needle with a metal detector?

WHAT YOU'LL NEED:

- ☐ I small AM transistor radio
- ☐ I small solar powered calculator
- ☐ I plastic CD jewel case
- ☐ 7-8 adhesive Velcro strips
- ☐ I piece of cardboard
- ☐ I pair of scissors
- ☐ Glue
- ☐ I broomstick

GLUE

DO NOT EAT

2.5 NET OZS

TIME REQUIRED: 20 minutes

WHAT TO DO:

In this experiment, you'll use the radio as a receiver of radio signals. The calculator emits a radio signal that your radio can pick up, which makes a tone. If you position these 2 objects so you can barely hear the noise generated by the calculator, that noise will be amplified if the radio waves come close to metal. *Voilà!* Metal detector.

STEP 1 You'll use the CD jewel case to hold your calculator and radio at a specific distance from each other. Cut 2 matching pieces of Velcro about 3 inches in length. Attach one to the back of the calculator and one to the back of the radio. Place the matching pieces of Velcro on the inside of the CD case. Then attach the radio and calculator with the Velcro to the inside of the case so they're facing each other.

STEP 2 Turn on the radio and make sure it's set to AM frequencies. Tune it to the highest possible frequency and find a spot where all you hear is static. Turn on the calculator. Close the CD case, bringing the calculator and radio closer to each other until you hear a loud tone. This is the radio receiving the radio wave from the calculator. Open the case again until you can just barely hear this tone.

STEP 3 Use the glue along the seam of the CD case to keep it in this position. You can also glue a piece of cardboard to the inside of the case to prop it open. While it dries, bring a piece of metal, like a coin, close to the detector. See what happens. How close does the coin need to be for the metal detector to react to it?

STEP 4 When the glue is dry, you can use another piece of Velcro to attach the metal detector to the end of a broomstick. Place one side of a Velcro strip on the broomstick and the other on the outside of the CD case. (This part is optional. It's fine to hold the detector in your hands and use it that way if you prefer.)

You're ready to go looking for buried treasure . . . or maybe just a needle in a haystack.

INDEX: